Jr. 3:30

I Love You
THIS MUCH

Experiencing the Satisfaction
of True Love in Marriage

Brian Edwards

CROSSBOOKS
PUBLISHING

CrossBooks™
A Division of LifeWay
1663 Liberty Drive
Bloomington, IN 47403
www.crossbooks.com
Phone: 1-866-879-0502

First published by CrossBooks 11/05/2012

ISBN: 978-1-4627-2287-7 (sc)
ISBN: 978-1-4627-2286-0 (e)
ISBN: 978-1-4627-2288-4 (hc)

Printed in the United States of America

Library of Congress Control Number: 2012920517

This book is printed on acid-free paper.

I Love You This Much **is dedicated to my wife, Denise.** Denise, twenty-three years ago I stood at an altar and said, "I do." I said those words because I couldn't imagine my life without you. Since that day there have been times of joy, times of brokenness, and thankfully, times of healing. We rejoiced together when our three daughters were born; we wept together when some of our precious loved ones left us for heaven. We've stood together through difficult trials and enjoyed God's greatest blessings together. We've been together so long it's hard for me to remember when we weren't together. A lot has changed since 1989, but there is one thing that hasn't changed: we're together. I don't know what the future holds or what we will face, but I know I want to walk through life, together.

CONTENTS

ACKNOWLEDGMENTS

I want to thank my dear friend Alan Dalton for encouraging me to write down what he still refers to as "The 4 S's of Love." As a photographer, he is constantly interacting with brides and grooms, and he never fails to share these simple principles. To meet a man in today's culture who places his marriage second only to his walk with God is refreshing. Alan Dalton Photography also did an amazing job on the cover photo, and for that I am extremely grateful.

I also want to express my appreciation to Barry and Kristin Harris for posing in the perfect way, at the perfect place for a remarkably beautiful picture. It's encouraging to know the love they have for each other and the real desire they have to honor God in their marriage.

I would also like to express my deepest gratitude for the tireless work Jack Faughn dedicated to this project. He masterfully handled the hard job of editing. This wasn't an easy project for him, but he faithfully dedicated hours of his time to make *I Love You This Much* better than I ever could have alone.

I would also like to thank my parents, as well as my wife's parents, for demonstrating what a life-long marriage looks like. Seeing their commitment to each other definitely impacted my view of marriage. Growing up with no insecurity about my Dad and Mom's relationship was a valuable contribution to my future. There were also times when Denise might have thrown in the towel were it not for the beliefs her parents instilled in her about "for better or for worse." I love and appreciate the godly heritage that has been passed down to us, and I pray that Denise and I will pass that down to our children as well.

Endorsements

Those of us who have heard Brian Edwards preach know that he is passionate about his message and he wants you to share his enthusiasm. You are also about to discover that Brian is passionate about marriage – his own and yours! Through personal stories and practical insights he will offer a way out of a stale marriage. He will reveal how you can experience the maximum relationship God offers to His children who are willing to pursue a love second only to His own. I don't think the book comes with a money-back guarantee but you won't need it anyway! Read slowly. Think deeply. Return to your first love (Brian will explain).

Frank P. Scurry
President
Carolina Graduate School of Divinity

IN THIS CULTURE OF DIVORCE, WE CANNOT HAVE ENOUGH VOICES SPEAKING TRUTH ABOUT MARRIAGE, Pastor Brian Edwards is such a voice. Every marriage would benefit from reading *I Love You This Much*.

Walter Shepherd
Director of Marriage Ministry
Osborne Baptist Church
Eden, NC

Some people are gifted communicators. Others are gifted counselors or pastors. But only the rare few are able to bring these gifts together in written form. Brian Edwards' book on love and marriage has done just that. The clarity, warmth, and wisdom that he displays in his book will surely help restore countless marriages and teach our country the true meaning of love.

Doug Bender
Graduate of Liberty University and Dallas Theological Seminary
Author of *I Am Second* and *Live Second*

This book is exactly what our world of struggling marriages needs to hear today, a simple, in touch explanation of God's design for marriage and a call to not settle for anything less. "I Love You This Much" explains the original principles of marriage in a fresh, engaging way that will bring help, hope and healing to its readers.

Lance Cook
Pastor/Teacher
Calvary Chapel
La Habra, CA

The institution of marriage is constantly under attack in our culture. I Love You This Much will equip you with the necessary tools to fight off these attacks. It will also help you in your quest to experience everything God has for you in the institution of marriage that He created. Brian's fresh and relevant perspective makes I Love You This Much a must read.

Mark Neal
Lead Pastor/planter
Oasis Baptist Church
Las Vegas, Nevada

Brian's Request

How can one person fix a marriage? The answer is simple—one person can't! I have performed hundreds of wedding ceremonies, and all of them have involved two people. You can't even have a wedding ceremony without two people, and you can't exchange vows or exchange rings without two people. There can't be a pronouncement of marriage without two people, and there definitely can't be an exciting honeymoon without two people. Everything about a marriage involves two people. However, I can't begin to count the times a concerned husband or wife has scheduled a counseling appointment with me to talk about marriage and then arrived for the appointment alone.

Please don't misunderstand. I respect their willingness to try and I appreciate their good intentions, but since two people are involved in the marriage, two people will have to be a part of the solution. That is why I am sincerely requesting that husbands and wives read *I Love You This Much* together. Whether it's over a cup of coffee in the morning or lying side by side at night doesn't matter, but what does matter is reading it *together.* I even intentionally limited the size of the book to increase the possibility that it would be read together. The principles in the book are so true that anyone who reads them and applies them will benefit, but the impact could be doubled by simply doubling the audience. Why not try to be creative and make your reading time special? Cuddling on the couch, having a picnic on the back deck, or sitting in a Starbuck's sharing your favorite coffee may make the journey through the upcoming pages something wonderful. I greatly appreciate anyone who takes the time to read the following chapters, but it would mean so much more for your marriage if you would simply read them together.

INTRODUCTION

Love …What is it? How do you truly experience it? How do you know it's real? Our culture makes these questions extremely difficult to answer. The reality is that love in our culture has been hijacked. Hallmark advertises love as a card. The romantic comedy creates a storyline of two unlikely people stumbling into the perfect relationship, the latest box office hit presents love as a sexually charged, constantly exciting, overly dramatic, all-consuming relationship filled with earth-shattering adventure. The problem is none of these look anything like reality. You will never convince your wife to climb through the windshield, grip the hood of your car, and fire a machine gun while you speed down the highway at one hundred miles per hour. It's also unrealistic to expect a passionate kiss while you completely ignore the pain of multiple gunshot wounds, and unfortunately the overindulgent Hallmark card will never perfectly describe your love life. The latest chart-topping love song, *Cosmopolitan*'s most recent "finding true love in ten easy steps" article, eHarmony's promise to help you find lasting love, none of these are true because none of these really have anything to do with true love. They are all usually based on this media-created fantasy that causes people to feel shortchanged in their marriages and unfulfilled by their mates. It's this fantasy that drives people to destroy their lives and the lives of their children by pursuing something that doesn't even exist.

Our culture makes it obvious that if love were a bull's-eye, most of our arrows would be landing somewhere on the fringes or missing the target completely. At some point, you have to wonder if people are familiar with the real thing. Some time ago, I read the testimony of a Secret Service agent who revealed that being trained to recognize a counterfeit involved intense study of the real thing. The agent said he had never personally seen a counterfeit, but that his intimate knowledge of the real would make the fake recognizable. People are really confused about love because they're not familiar with the real thing, and they never consult the creator of love. They mindlessly go through life and relationships, never stopping to realize the fulfillment they desperately long for can only be found through God.

So before we dive into the sea of this huge subject, let's first make sure we completely understand how to recognize true love. Thankfully, God defines that for us in 1 Corinthians 13. He says through Paul, "Love is." Those two words alone should captivate our attention if our goal is to know what love is. Imagine for just a moment how awesome it would be to focus the attention of the millions of people who are searching for love on those two words, "Love is." Those two words scream to a world living in confusion, "The search is over, you can know the truth!" Not a distorted view of truth, but *truth*. Yet people continue to crowd the "self-help" aisles at the local bookstore without even realizing the true definition of love is found in the pages of the Bible. This definition is from God and it clearly defines love, so continue reading while remembering 2 Timothy 3:16: "All Scripture is given by inspiration of God." Also be careful to notice as you read that love is more about characteristics than emotions. These aren't emotions that can exist if a person is in love, but characteristics that will accompany and evince true love.

> Love is patient, love is kind, love is not jealous, love
> is not boastful, it is not proud or rude. Love does

not demand its own way. Love is not irritable and does not keep a record when it has been wronged. It does not rejoice in evil, but rejoices in truth. Love bears all things, believes all things, endures all things, love never fails. (1 Corinthians 13:4–8, author's paraphrase)

This would be a great time to take a moment, examine yourself, your relationship, and your marriage. After a thorough investigation, honestly identify how many of these characteristics are nonexistent in your relationship. Ask yourself, as a husband, "How many of these characteristics are modeled in me?" Ask yourself, as a wife, "How many of these characteristics are displayed in my daily life?" How patient are you with your spouse? How often do you search for opportunities to be kind to your spouse? Are you irritable, are you quick-tempered, or do you keep a record of your spouse's mistakes for leverage or manipulation? These are the kind of questions you need to ask yourself under extreme personal scrutiny. After reading God's description of love, it's obvious that the majority of the married world is currently living without true love. That explains why so many marriages quickly deteriorate and others merely exist due to a feeling of obligation. It reveals why so many people wear a ring on the third finger of their left hand, but continue to search and even long for something more.

I Love You This Much is more than words on a page. Each chapter is a glimpse into my personal story, and each paragraph represents the lessons I've learned over the course of my marriage. Hopefully in the pages of this small book you will be able to discover what true love is, so that you will better recognize what true love is not. My hope is that you will sit down as a couple and devote the few minutes that reading this book will require. It would also be extremely beneficial if you would take a few moments to talk after each chapter and discover where you're succeeding and possibly uncover where you're failing. Trust me, I know how difficult a revealing conversation can be, but I also know compassionate communication can be extremely rewarding. Please know this book has been prayed over, and my prayer is that your love life will be radically transformed by God's power.

CHAPTER 1:
Love Is Sacrificial

I f you could author your own definition of love would it include sacrifice? Maybe your initial response is, "Of course not!" People usually avoid that word—even more so they avoid that practice as often as possible. Sacrifice costs too much, it's too inconvenient, and it involves giving rather than getting. All of these facts make the idea of sacrifice extremely problematic in our culture. After all, who wants to sacrifice? The people we admire most in our society are the people who have it all. Their images are plastered on every magazine cover; their luxurious lifestyles are constantly put on display, causing average Americans to struggle with raging envy. This has shaped the way we think. We have become a culture consumed with receiving, not giving. Our lustful emotions have led this generation to be described as the "least generous generation in our nation's history."[1] The notion of sacrifice seems completely ludicrous—maybe you're thinking even now, "Not me, I'm not interested in sacrifice. I'm willing to give some as long as my spouse doesn't expect too much." The problem is, real love can't exist apart from sacrifice. The words *love* and *sacrifice* are eternally married. They're so intertwined that they can't be separated. It is completely impossible to have one without the other.

Dr. Gary Smalley, nationally known writer and marriage authority, described sacrificial love in these words: "Being a servant in marriage is putting your mate first—even above yourself—and giving yourself for the other…. It's saying, I promise to make you more important than me. I promise to put your needs above my own. I promise to give up my preferences and even my needs if it serves your well-being."[2] You *can* have true love without a fairytale wedding, an island honeymoon, the perfect home in a cul-de-sac, a dog and two children, but you *can't* have true love without sacrifice.

It is interesting to me that the opening words of the Bible are a love story. It begins with God fashioning dust in the form of a man. Dirt became flesh and experienced life as God breathed life into lifeless nostrils. Adam stood for the first time with an instinctive awareness of God and was given authority by God, but although Adam had authority over God's creation and a life without stress, need, or fear he still had a deep inward longing for companionship. Something inside of him yearned to live his life with someone else. Without a meaningful relationship his life felt empty and unfulfilled. Until recently I had never fully grasped the significance of the word "alone." How could the Bible say Adam was alone? I would always default to, "Adam wasn't alone, he had God," but it was God who acknowledged Adam's loneliness. God knew that Adam needed a suitable companion because it was God who had placed that desire in Adam's heart. It was God who had designed man with the desire for an intimate relationship. God knew that Adam needed a wife. He needed someone who would complete him, who would hide his weaknesses in their strengths, who would affirm him and sexually satisfy him. God's answer to Adam's issues of loneliness was Eve. God, physician and creator, performed a divine surgery by extracting one rib from Adam's side. With the bone God selected, He made a beautiful statement about love. It wasn't a bone from Adam's head, nor was it a bone from Adam's foot, but it was a bone located next to Adam's heart—which is exactly where a woman should be held by the man who loves her. With that one rib God did something only God could do – He formed something as visually appealing as a woman.

Imagine how Adam must have felt when he woke up and saw Eve—completely unclothed and unashamed. All Adam had ever seen was a bunch of dirty, hairy animals. Elephants, donkeys, and monkeys really weren't that attractive. He had never seen anything as remarkable, as perfectly sculpted as Eve. No wonder his first statement involved the words, "She will be my..." Finally his feelings of loneliness were erased by feelings of satisfaction and love.

However, Adam's love for his wife wasn't proven by his appreciation of her beauty or his obsession with the sound of her voice, but his love was proven by his selfless act of sacrifice. The day Eve ate the fruit she was completely deceived by Satan, the master of deception. She really believed she could eat the fruit without consequence. In her mind she was one bite away from being like God. Finally she could be like the one they admired and worshipped. Unfortunately, her catastrophic decision resulted in the immediate loss of her innocence, which exposed her sin. Adam knew full well that meant God's promise of death would be a reality in Eve's life.

Imagine the weight of his dilemma. He could abandon Eve, condemn her for her actions, and maintain his place in the garden. That decision would tear him away from his wife but allow him to keep his close relationship with God.

Or he could sin.

That decision would cause him to lose his life, his relationship with God, his innocence, his stress-free existence, but allow him to continue to live in oneness with Eve. This was a dilemma of epic proportions. Adam decided in that tragic moment that his devotion to his wife meant more than his relationship with God. The conversation that took place that day between this husband and wife isn't recorded in the Bible. There had to be tears shed as Adam witnessed his wife losing her innocence and being separated from God. The question could have even been raised by Eve, "What about us, Adam?" The truth is we don't know, but Adam could have easily said to Eve before he took his bite of the forbidden fruit, "I love you this much, so much that I'm willing to sacrifice everything for you." Adam wasn't deceived. He ate the fruit with his eyes wide open (1 Timothy 2:14).

The Scripture never says that Adam craved the fruit or desired to be like God. How long had Adam lived in the garden before Eve? That question can't be answered, but we can say with certainty that he had never eaten the fruit before. There is no record that Satan had even attempted to lure him toward the tree. John Gill says in his exposition of the Bible, "Adam was never deceived at all; neither by the serpent, with whom he never conversed; nor by his wife, he knew what he did … he took and ate out of love to his wife, from a fond affection of her, to bear her company, and that she might not die alone."[3] Adam heard what God said about eating the forbidden fruit. I'm sure those words were fresh in his mind, "for in the day that you eat of it you shall surely die" (Genesis 2:17).

Adam was not divine. He didn't comprehend that eating the fruit would cause immediate spiritual death and eventually lead to physical death. He couldn't see into the future. He didn't know the devastation his rebellious decision would cause. Remember, the moment he made his decision he was still sinless, he was still innocent. Sadly, sin quickly erased his innocence and caused him to be driven by selfishness. His decision to place Eve before God immediately changed who he was and how he behaved. Moments after eating the fruit he stood *beside* Eve, but not *with* Eve. He blamed his wife before God in an attempt to excuse his own actions, but that was *after* sin. One second *before* he bit the fruit he was still innocent. In that moment he only knew his wife had sinned and was destined to die. He only knew he didn't want to live without her. It was that selfless act of sacrifice that proved Adam's love for Eve.

God calls men to love their wives in this way. Not that we would follow them into sin or place them before God, but that we would be willing to give ourselves for them. He communicates that through these words: "Husbands, love your wives, just as Christ also loved the church, and gave Himself for her" (Ephesians 5:25). Jesus' sacrifice is our example. God doesn't call the husband to prove his love by giving his wife a car, a house, or a shopping allowance, but instead God mandates that our love be proven by our level of sacrifice. What an incredible weight of responsibility! We are the leaders of our homes, so God doesn't offer us the convenient option of waiting to react after measuring our wives' levels of giving. Instead he calls us to create an example of giving by modeling sacrificial love. God requires that husbands follow the example of His Son. Jesus' life was a continual demonstration of sacrifice. His very existence on the earth testified of His commitment to give without limits. His first breath as an infant was taken in a stable that was polluted by the animals that were kept there. How fitting that the Lamb of God started His earthly journey in a stable. There was no royal palace for Him. He was here to serve. His ministry would begin with His baptism and quickly be dominated by continual acts of service. Once He walked down from the mountain of temptation He began the most demanding public ministry in history. Reading through the Gospels I can't help but feel sympathy for Jesus. The weight of redeeming the world was on His shoulders. His grueling schedule pushed Him to point of exhaustion. The crowds demanded His attention, not even realizing that each time He healed their sicknesses He was giving of Himself. Jesus was so committed to compassion that He journeyed for hours from the mountains of Decapolis to the Coast of Tyre and Sidon just to help one desperate woman. He walked out of His way to meet a promiscuous woman who had been rejected by society so He could forgive her sins. He was without food for three days in the wilderness, but He broke bread and fish so He could satisfy the hunger of the multitude. Throughout the Gospels, one account after another reveals the never-ending sacrifice of Jesus. He sacrificed His time, He sacrificed His comfort and He sacrificed His life. This is our example. That means there is no room for a sense of entitlement, no room for the couch-sitting, TV-remote-controlling television addict who feels his wife exists to cater to his every wish. The husband who follows the example of Jesus is a husband who's willing to crucify his selfish motives in order to give life to sacrificial love.

The wife who is blessed to have a husband like this should always respond with her own personal commitment to sacrificial love in order to combat the tendency to take sacrificial love for granted, which is a serious offence. Love taken for granted is eventually love destroyed. A wife who is practicing sacrificial love sees her husband's needs as an opportunity rather than an obligation. She meets his sexual, emotional, and relational needs through her generosity as she willingly gives to him sacrificially. She lovingly admires him; she graciously supports him, and prayerfully strengthens him to be the man that God desires him to be.

The couple who experiences this love experiences happiness

and fulfillment that very few people will ever know. One author suggested sacrifice should be nonexistent in marriage.[4] In his opinion, sacrifice would lead to unhappiness. I believe just the opposite. Sacrifice leads to real satisfaction, and this is the truth most couples never discover. Marriage is about more than our happiness. Ultimately it is about the glory of God, and sacrificial love glorifies Him (John 15:13). The measure of your love for each other is proven by the level of your sacrifice. Unfortunately, this is the vital ingredient that most marriages are without, and it's the one ingredient you have to have in order to achieve a successful marriage. Selfish ambitions, motives, and agendas all act as thieves, stealing fulfillment in a marriage relationship. Charles Mylander said in his book *The Christ-Centered Marriage*, "Selfishness will kill any marriage! Selflessness by both spouses makes for a good marriage, and both husband and wife will be satisfied."[5] When you faced your spouse at the altar and declared "I do," you were declaring your intention to invest your life in meeting the needs of your spouse. Two become one, or I could say, two become first. Neither the husband nor the wife dominates the marriage by demanding their needs be fulfilled at the expense of their spouse's needs being met. A marriage that honors God is a marriage where both husband and wife live to put each other first.

Not long ago my wife and I sat holding hands at a local diner when my friend Blair slid into the booth next to me. With tears in his eyes he said to both of us, "You had better enjoy and appreciate this because it won't last forever." He started by reminding us that he was eighty years old and then quickly followed that with, "And you know I don't have my wife anymore." He then shared with a beautiful openness the story of their sixty-year marriage. With a gleam in his eyes he said, "It was so perfect I wouldn't have changed anything. We laughed, we flirted, we always held hands, we always made over each other, and now that she's gone my life will never be the same." He then closed his story by sharing her painful battle with Alzheimer's and how he never left her side. His love for her ran so deep that even in her absence she was still being loved. As he left our table he looked at me and said, "You live every day trying to do more for her than she's done for you." Then, looking at my wife Denise, he said, "You live every day trying to do more for him than he's done for you." He then said with a calm confidence, "And you will always have a happy marriage."

I agree with Blair. His philosophy couldn't be any truer. If I had the opportunity to say one thing to you about love, it would be this: "It is impossible to love selfishly." If this were a text message I would write the phrase in all caps: "IT IS IMPOSSIBLE TO LOVE SELFISHLY." By the end of the book I hope you realize this: it is impossible to love selfishly.

When you hear that phrase it seems simple, but I believe it's the deepest truth God has ever revealed regarding love. It's such a powerful principle that God even applies it to Himself. He can create the world, He can breathe into nostrils made of dust and initiate life, He can exist eternally without changing, He can even measure the waters of the Earth in the hollow of His hand, but He cannot love selfishly. God, the infinite all-powerful, was required to sacrifice in order to express His love. "For God so loved the world." So what's He going to do about it? If He really loves the world how is He going to prove it? "[T]hat He gave His only begotten Son" (John 3:16). "He who did not spare His own Son, but delivered Him up for us all" (Romans 8:32).

God's love is so clearly demonstrated through His sacrifice

that it dispels the question, "Am I loved by God?" Of course you are loved by God—look how much He was willing to sacrifice for you! True love doesn't say, "I'm going to get mine," true love doesn't manipulate circumstances in order to be on the receiving end of generosity, but true love sacrifices because that's what true love does. The image of Jesus hanging on a cross, giving of Himself until there was nothing left to give, should be our image of true love. If you want to see true love read the last five chapters of John's Gospel. It's more than a song that conjures up sentimental emotions and it's more than a movie that gives you a momentary reprieve from reality. It's a real commitment before God to love someone else enough to give to them sacrificially. This can only be done through Jesus. I pray that as you close this chapter you will establish Jesus as the role model of your marriage, and that you will earnestly seek to follow Him to a deeper level of sacrificial love.

CHAPTER 2:
Love Is Securing

arriage has serious enemies.

Some of them viciously attack, leaving behind only the carnage of a destroyed relationship. Others act slowly, and like a cancer they secretively erode the strength of a healthy relationship. Virtually everyone could correctly list the most common problems that cause marriages to fail. Adultery, financial issues, abuse, and neglect typically find their place at the top of the list, but for some reason people frequently overlook one of marriage's most serious enemies. It probably wouldn't even make the list, yet it has the potential to drive an immoveable wedge between the happiest husband and wife. This enemy is called insecurity.

True love offers the greatest level of security available in a world dominated by insecurity. True love offers acceptance, confidence, safety, and assurance. None of these are optional. They all have to exist in a healthy marriage. No one can survive for a prolonged period of time in an environment of constant uncertainty. Even the notion that insecurity would exist in a marriage is opposite God's design. Marriage, when functioning correctly, produces confidence, security, and stability. A person's self-worth is consistently affirmed by a loving spouse who frequently encourages the one he or she loves. However, when one spouse feels the pain of inferiority, the coldness of rejection, and a longing for acceptance, insecurity emerges and creates doubts about self-worth. This spouse is usually easy to identify because they are constantly trying to produce an action impressive enough to capture the heart of the one they love. The person who *should* represent this husband or wife's priceless treasure *instead* represents their never ending quest. This spouse lives in hope that one day all the giving, loving and trying will cause an indifferent husband or wife to respond with expressions of securing love. Serious damage is caused when a husband or wife has to pursue a heart that should already belong to them. The spouse who's caught in this cycle eventually empties his or her emotional bank account—only to be left emptier and more insecure than ever before. I've counseled the wife who always plans the special occasions and attempts to create the memorable romantic moments. She's the one who always reserves the hotel room, makes the dinner reservation, and writes the meaningful card. She's the one who goes against her better judgment and risks being disappointed again. I've also counseled the husband who pours himself out for an unappreciative wife. He caresses her, compliments her, and attempts to romance her. He spends time with her, listens to her, and adores her. Deep inside he hopes one day she'll cherish him and pour herself out for him. More often than not that never happens. Sadly, I've witnessed how badly a broken-hearted spouse hurts. I've sat and talked with the wife who cries because she feels discarded or unimportant. I've listened to the husband who shares the brokenness of his heart as tears flow down his face. By the time these spouses reach my office they're empty, they're extremely bitter and wanting answers to their long list of questions: "Why won't my spouse love me like I love him/her?", "What have I done to deserve this?", "Why am I not good enough?", "Why doesn't he or she want to be with me?" All of these questions haunt the mind of the person who's gripped in the vice of insecurity.

I warn the spouse tempted to dismiss himself or herself from the guilt of contributing to the insecurity of his or her husband or wife to *reject that temptation*. Living in disobedience to your marital responsibility is sin, and God never takes sin lightly. Scripture clearly says, "The wages of sin is death" (Romans 6:23). Like a savage beast, sin assaults *all* of our relationships, including our marriages, and when tolerated the result is always death. The only antidote for sin is repentance, and true repentance emerges after we respond to conviction. The awareness of our rebellion produces a nagging discomfort that forces us to live life in a different way. Repentance is more than confessing, it's accepting the blame and following through with all the necessary steps to experience freedom (Psalm 51).

Wife, God Himself created, called and designed you to complete your husband. You were never designed to empty him of personal self-worth or manipulate him into submission. I know you feel like it's your calling to help God mold him and make him into the man you—I mean *He* needs him to be—but it's not. You were designed to complete him, and when you live to complete your husband you are the crown jewel of his life (Proverbs 12:4). Husband, God has called and ordained you to honor your wife. You were never designed to empty her of personal self-worth or treat her as an unequal partner. God calls you to honor her by treating her like a rare, fragile vessel that deserves special attention (1 Peter 3:7).

According to Scripture, you are to value your wife more than you would value a costly jewel (Proverbs 31:10). She's not the "old lady"! She's not the "old gray mare"! And before you open your mouth to talk about what's drooped and what's expanded on her, look in the mirror for what's shrunken and what's flopped on you. Adore her, praise her, and cherish her. This is right, and when it's lived out it's incredibly beautiful. A husband and wife who honor and cherish each other become a living portrait of true love.

> To honor someone means to give them respect and high esteem, to treat them as being special and of great worth. When you speak to them, you keep your language clean and understandable. You are courteous and polite. When they speak to you, you take them seriously, giving their words weight and significance. When they ask you to do something, you accommodate them if at all possible, simply out of respect for who they are." (*The Love Dare*)[6]
> This is what God desires for us to experience. Being true to His design for our marriages ensures that we will honor and cherish and be honored and cherished.

A man is validated by a wife who needs his attention, and a wife is validated by a husband who gives attention to her needs. A man's need for admiration (honor) is one of the greatest needs in his life. Jimmy and Karen Evans said in their bestselling book *Marriage on the Rock*, "Men are all the same in one area: they all need honor. (We didn't say they want honor. We said they need it.) In fact, honor is a man's foremost need."[7] While these words are true, I realize there are times when it isn't easy to honor your husband. Sometimes he may not seem very honorable. Men do have moments, and by moments I mean moments that aren't pretty. Unfortunately, I know this from experience. It will require you to stretch your imagination to believe this, but, wait for it... I'm not perfect. I proved that several years ago when my wife sent me out to our storage building to carry in a small, glass-top entertainment center. My masculinity made me her obvious choice to do the job (not really). I was actually her only choice, but duty called and I answered. I finally found the entertainment center, picked it up, and headed back to our house. Just as I started across the yard with this heavy entertainment center in my arms, I heard her call out, "Somebody wants you on the phone."

Now, you have to understand my wife is unwilling to say the words "Can he call you back later?" or "Will you please hold?" But no, the moment the phone rings she goes sergeant on me and expects me to march straight in and take the call. I knew that, but since I was being a good husband and carrying in the entertainment center I thought I would try, "Find out who it is and tell them I'll call them back later." She responded, "But I don't know who it is and they want to speak to you."

It was at that moment that I started mumbling to myself, "Why can't she ever just take a message? What part of 'I'm busy right now' is she not getting?" I might have been just a little mad when I shoved the entertainment center to the ground, but that didn't come close to how mad I was the moment the glass top flung open and cut my face. At that moment it didn't matter that I was in the front yard, it didn't matter that every single one of our neighbors was mowing their grass. I picked the entertainment center up off the ground, lifted it over my head, and slammed it down as hard as I could. Then I started jumping up and down on it until I broke it into a thousand pieces.

While all of this insanity was going on, my wife was standing on the front porch of our house and she wasn't shouting, "I honor you, Brian! You're an amazing husband! You are so cool!" She was actually shouting, "What in the world are you doing—have you lost your mind?" If my wife based honoring me on my less than perfect moments, she wouldn't honor me. If she pressed the pause button and stayed at that point in time, or resurrected that moment in all of our conversations, she would never honor me. The point is, your husband isn't perfect and he never will be. There will always be moments when he's not very honorable, but think about how often he deserves to be honored. Also try to remember that he *needs* you to honor him, and instead of constantly reminding him of his faults, praise his successes. Accept that God calls you to honor him because he's your husband. Wife, it isn't enough that he is honored at work as a successful employee or that he's honored as a father by your children. He needs to be honored by you.

A woman's need for security (comfort) is often considered the greatest need in her life. This is not a weakness in her – it is a need! Women are amazingly strong. A few moments in labor and delivery prove their strength. If childbirth were the responsibility of men the human race would have been extinct a long time ago. Women successfully work hours outside of the home, and still find the strength and dedication to care for their families. Women are capable, intelligent, and resourceful, but that doesn't change their need for security. Regardless of their strength they still need to be consoled and compassionately loved. Highly respected speaker and author Gary Smalley says in his book, *If Only He Knew*, "A woman loves to build a lasting relationship with a man who cares about her enough to let her lean on him when she needs comfort."[8] Husband, your responsibility is to protect and care for your wife. Your calling is to assure your wife that she is secure— regardless of the circumstances surrounding her. God designed her to need this, and He designed you to provide it.

Once we understand these needs, we understand that both men and women crave some form of affirmation. The call to abolish insecurity from our marriages is clearly heard when we listen to the truth. These two very real needs are also directly connected to our really big need to feel significant; *the things that are significant in your life are the things that really matter.* All people have an inward desire to feel like they matter to someone else. It's okay. You're not the only one with the desire to feel significant, *and there shouldn't be anywhere you feel more significant than in your marriage relationship.*

Jesus communicated the importance of significance in a conversation He had with His bride, the Church in Ephesus (Revelation 2:1–7). It was a revealing conversation about an invisible, virtually undetectable problem. As you read through the verses, it's easy to criticize this church for a failure to love Jesus, but it wasn't a case of their love for Jesus being nonexistent. It wasn't that its members didn't love Jesus at all, but it was an issue of first love. For years I taught these verses incorrectly, only repeating what I had heard said over and over again about them. Even recently I've heard a few of America's most famous pastors make the same mistake I made in the past, accusing this church of "losing" their first love. Read the verses and it's obvious that "losing" had nothing to do with Jesus' conversation with His bride. The marriage between them wasn't suffering because of misplaced love, and teaching the verse in that way is an enormous error. Jesus clearly said to the Ephesian Church, "You have *left* your first love" (verse 4, emphasis added). He never said anything about them losing their love for Him. So why would Pastors and Bible teachers replace the word "left" with the word "lost?" The word "lost" never appears anywhere in the verse, but the word "left" does. Jesus' conversation was clearly about leaving.

Why then has the content of the verse been changed? I asked that question and eventually realized the answer is connected to our need to justify our actions. We want to be innocent. We want to be able to blame our actions on someone or something else. That makes everything more comfortable. We justify the subtle sins in our lives by calling them accidents. We all know that losing something is completely accidental. No one intentionally misplaces something so he or she can waste hours of their lives searching for what was intentionally lost. Losing something happens when we get distracted or stressed. It happens when we have too much on our minds, or we have too much on our plates to keep up with one more thing. It's an oversight. We accidentally lose things, and our reaction is, "Don't be too critical because, after all, everyone has accidents."

A few years ago my family was in a busy Walmart. Two of our three daughters were hiding in the clothes, running down the aisles, and wreaking havoc. Since my wife was on a mission to buy some things we needed, my job was to keep up with the kids. It sounds like a simple job but it's not. If you're the parent of at least three children, you realize that's easier said than done. Somehow during chasing them around, yelling like a madman, and being totally frustrated by the fact they weren't listening to me, I lost sight of our youngest daughter. At that moment I was living a parent's nightmare. As a parent, you know the meltdown you experience when you're gripped by the fear of losing your child. Frantically I looked up and down the aisles. Over and over again I called out her name, but she wouldn't respond. Finally I came running to my wife and said, "Honey, come quickly! I can't find Marley!" I was furious when my wife didn't budge. I said, "If you could stop shopping for one minute and care more about our child than whatever it is you're looking for, that would be good!" Once again she ignored my urgency and continued looking through the items hanging on the rack. It was as if she didn't care. Finally I asked, "Why don't you care that I can't find Marley!" She responded, "Because you're holding her." I looked on my left hip, and sure enough there she was, sitting in complete silence. She even thought it was funny that I thought she was lost. I didn't think it was funny at all.

While I'm not a mind reader, I'm almost sure that I know what you're thinking right now ("What an idiot!"), and trust me, that's exactly how I felt. What happened that evening in that crowded Walmart was the result of me being completely distracted by three children, an in-depth conversation with someone on my cell phone, and the masses of people who were shopping around me. It was just more than I could effectively handle. There were too many distractions, and in that moment I thought I had lost something —well, *someone*. That's not at all what's being communicated in Jesus' conversation with the Ephesian Church. If my night at Walmart were being written about in Revelation, the storyline wouldn't be the same. Instead of being distracted and confused, I would have *intentionally* left my children for the shopping, for the crowd, and for the phone conversation. Ephesus wasn't *accidentally* distracted. They were actually guilty of loving other things more than they loved Jesus. They "left" their first love. Jesus was no longer first in their lives. They made a deliberate choice to make other things more meaningful than their relationship with Him.

Communicating the message that "first love is lost" has to be considered bad—*really bad*. It allows people to use an excuse to get off the hook. Sure, they may take a few moments to feel guilty, but ultimately they place the blame on their busy lives, their lack of time, or how distracted they've been due to all of their respon-sibilities. Never mind that most of the things now referred to as responsibilities are really nothing more than unnecessary add-ons that are treated as necessary. A quick prayer of "I'm sorry" and the person guilty of "leaving their first love" places that sin in the file of things they've already dealt with. The problem is they really haven't dealt with the sin they've committed. Leaving your first love is not a simple accident that only requires an "I'm sorry." It's a deliberate act of walking away. Jesus was describing people who deliberately, intentionally, and consciously walked away, leaving behind their first love. The question is, "How did that happen to the church in Ephesus?" Or maybe a better question would be, "How is it we're guilty of doing the same thing?"

We know Jesus should be the preeminent love of our lives, and still we blatantly walk away from the love we know should be first. How could we ever allow something so wrong to happen in our own lives? How does someone consciously leave love? How does someone who was willing to abandon their personal identity and relinquish all the freedom of being single just walk away? What causes people who willingly participated in a wedding—and even exchanged sacred vows—to reach the point that they allow themselves to feel totally unrestrained by any of those commit-ments? Some people try to make the devil their scapegoat by using the ever-popular, "The devil made me do it." How convenient is that? A person cheats on, abuses, or abandons his or her spouse and then simply places it all on the devil's account. Others blame their spouse, conveniently freeing themselves from taking any personal responsibility. The fact is we leave first love because we love something or someone else more. A more appealing apple catches our eye and then demands our love. It's all a matter of significance.

When we're dating we can't imagine there would be anything or anyone that could possibly be more significant than the one who's captivated our hearts. We have endless phone conversations that include at least three "no you hang up first" endings. Our plans always include time together. We live to see each other. We live with an intense desire to be together. We plan to spend the rest our lives with this person we feel we couldn't live without. We have to have them. All of that is prevalent in the atmosphere of our pre-marriage relationship.

During our dating years we're more likely to kiss more often, more likely to hold hands, more likely to make special occasions special, but for some reason that starts to change after the wedding. We rarely speak the words "I love you", moments of affection become infrequent, and the scales are shifted by all the things competing for our attention. The house we dreamed of has to be cleaned, the lawn has to be mowed, and all of that has to be significant. The jobs we have in order to pay the bills we create have to be considered significant. However, even those issues become insignificant when children arrive. Suddenly they captivate our attention and demand all our energy. We finally reach the place where we're exhausted by all the significant things in our lives. Our obligations place demands on us that are difficult to meet, and all of this leads to feelings of emptiness. Finally we're overwhelmed by the feeling that we have nothing left to give. Conversations and arguments revolve around "I'm tired" or "I can't do anything else," and accusations fly as we argue over who's pulling the majority of the weight. The people involved in this struggle used to be madly in love. They used to see their marriage as the most important part of their lives. If they would only stop and take inventory, they would realize the only *insignificant* thing is their marriage. They have made no adjustments in other areas to make time for their marriage, but they have repeatedly adjusted their marriage to make time for other things.

Eventually the couple I'm describing begins to discuss their feelings of emptiness and dissatisfaction. Symptoms such as decreased intimacy and infrequent communication are warning signs of a terminal disease that threatens to destroy their marriage. The couple who's trapped in this web typically blames each other for their failure. Their emptiness eventually drives them to seek satisfaction by walking away or falling into the arms of another person. It seems completely insane, but it's a scenario that is repeated over and over again, even by those who are in the church.

Ask these couples what went wrong and they will point to financial, sexual, emotional, or relational issues. The husband will blame his wife for her constant nagging or her endless excuses to avoid sex. The wife will blame her inattentive husband who never listens or attempts to make her feel special. She may even mention the man he used to be when they were dating. Neither one of them ever points to the things they invited into their lives. They never blame the things that became more significant than their love for each another. Eventually they see each another as unimportant and they grant themselves permission to leave. They don't even realize they've been on a journey that led them to marital insignificance. They question how they could possibly stay with someone they no longer love. How is it they forget how madly in love they once were? How do they forget the feelings that led them to the altar? The insignificance they feel in their marriage distorts those memories, and soon love is replaced by anger. Two people who once pledged their lives to each another leave their relationship, unable to be friends.

Please don't let this happen in your marriage.

Maintain your first love relationship. Don't forget that you loved each other before there was a house, before there were children, before there were all of the distractions. Don't be like Jesus' bride in Ephesus and walk away from your first love.

Some time back, I heard a well-known pastor make the statement "The road to destruction is paved with supposition." No one can survive in a constant state of guessing. A marriage can never be expected to thrive in an environment of insecurity. There has to be bedrock, and that foundational rock has to be an unwavering-beyond-any-doubt-love, the kind of love that assures your spouse that he or she is unquestionably significant. Couples that place Jesus first and remain constant in their pursuit of Him know the joy of true love. When a husband loves Jesus first, his love for his wife will never be called into question. When a wife loves Jesus first, her devotion to her marriage relationship never has to be called into question. Jesus said that if we seek Him first all other things will be added to us (Matthew 6:33). It's when Jesus assumes His rightful place of significance that everything and everyone else finds their rightful place.

David Clarke, an author and psychologist, said in his book *Kiss Me Like You Mean It*: "We've all had human passion, haven't we? Because it's fueled by human strength, it's weak and never lasts. God is the source of true passion in marriage. It comes from Him and only from Him."[9] It's true; God is the source of every good and perfect gift including marital passion. You can't be truly passionate about God and not be passionate about loving your spouse. I've never met a couple who struggled with marital insignificance that was effectively practicing *spiritual* significance. That is, living every aspect of life in light of Jesus. Living for "His name's sake" (Psalm 23:3). However, I have met people, some even in full-time ministry, who walked away from Jesus before walking away from their husband or wife. Marriage gives you such an amazing opportunity to demonstrate the glory of God to other people. It allows you to put on display Jesus' relationship with His bride the church. Being passionate about the glory and majesty of God is the centerpiece of a spiritually healthy marriage. Allow your marriage to shout to those around you, "God is first!"

When your spiritual life matters, your marital life will matter more. When you love God first, you love the things God loves *more*. Your only hope of experiencing true love is God. He is the one who teaches us the joy of esteeming others. When His love is present in your marriage, you will experience a deeper love for your spouse. Only God offers "perfect love" (1 John 4:18). Love without fear of abandonment, betrayal, or rejection. His love shows us what it feels like to have real security. Paul talked about God's love with confidence. He said, "Neither death nor life, nor angels, nor principalities, nor powers, nor things present nor things to come, nor height nor depth, nor any other created thing shall be able to separate us from the love of God which is in Christ Jesus our Lord" (Romans 8:38–39).

We all know we are not God, but my challenge to you is that you would strive to live out Godly love in your marriage. Gift your spouse with the confidence that nothing will ever separate them from your love. Assure them of their worth and then work to maintain your first love. The Church of Ephesus didn't guard their first love. There was a time when no other church was more committed than they were. No other church was more successful than they were and no other church was more passionate about Jesus than they were. Eventually that time disappeared. Other things captivated their hearts, and the things that didn't matter in the end cost them what mattered most. Leaving their first love resulted in them losing the security of God's presence.

Don't allow the absence of "first love" to rob your marriage of lasting love. Don't allow your marriage to become insignificant. If you have, change now! Start walking back to what you've walked away from. Erase the insecurity that threatens to destroy the heart of the person who loved you enough to say, "I do."

CHAPTER 3:
Love Is Shown

I f your spouse has to *wonder* whether or not you love them, *you don't!*

Think about that for a moment.

True love can't be hidden or contained. It always looks for opportunities to be revealed. Love isn't something you hold deep inside your heart completely out of sight, but it's something deep inside your heart that forces its way into your life's practices. It's more than a group of words, and simply saying, "I love you" doesn't make it so. True love produces actions –actions that assure your husband or wife that he or she is loved. That means true love is more than a feeling or a state of mind. As a matter of fact, if you really love someone it can be exhausting. A great example of this is the mother who adores her children, trying to maintain her sanity while taking them shopping for groceries. All it takes is one look and you realize she's hanging on by a thread. You recognize her by the overwhelming look of tiredness and frustration on her face. The children's hair is perfectly fixed and hers isn't, their clothes are immaculate and her shirt should have a graphic that reads, "KIDS have been here." However, the thing that always amazes me about her is that no matter how inconvenienced she is, or how frustrated she might be, she's putting her love on display by caring for her children. Through her awareness of her children's needs and her tireless effort to meet those needs, she loudly communicates her unconditional love for them. That's simply how love behaves. It doesn't wait for the right moment to make a grand entrance, but rather it consistently gives visible confirmation of its existence.

That kind of obvious love needs to be present in your marriage.

If you're thinking, "Well, I would *love* for my husband to show me that kind of love," or "I hope my wife is listening to what she's reading," you're missing it. The love I'm describing can only be achieved by a husband and wife who both wear the same jersey but work tirelessly as individuals to score the most points.

Recently I complimented my wife while some of our friends were close by. One of them asked, "Are you trying to score points?" My response was simply," Yes—I want to score all the points I possibly can!" Scoring points is not a bad thing. Marriage should be two people competing with each other to see who can score the most points by showing the greatest amount of love. A couple should willingly expend more energy in their marriage than a soccer team expends scoring a goal. And you should be ashamed if a football team burns more energy scoring a meaningless touchdown than you burn in winning the heart of your spouse.

I can almost hear some of you asking, "Really?" Yes, *really!* It's discouraging to hear husbands and wives assume that their spouses know that they are loved. Too many people are like the couple who filed for divorce after fifty-two years of marriage. The judge asked, "Why are you divorcing after so many years?" The wife responded, "Because he hasn't told me he loved me since our wedding day." The judge looked at the husband and asked, "Is this true – you haven't told your wife you love her in fifty-two years?" The husband responded, "I told her on our wedding day that I loved her and that if I ever changed my mind I would let her know." How sad is it that this is actually true in countless marriages? No work is ever invested, no creativity is ever employed, and no energy is ever expended. The marriage is dominated by laziness and the indifference of a husband or wife who doesn't see why that is a problem.

How sad is it that people invest more effort in their jobs than their spouses? That some men invest hours of energy and patience in their golf game, but only invest minutes into their wives? That wives invest hours on the computer or with the children or at their job, but never invest significant energy in their husbands? No wonder so many marriages end in divorce. Nine days before his death Winston Churchill said, "I'm so bored with it all."[10] If that describes your marriage there is a real problem. Love is never boring because love is an action. If you love, you will be love-*ing*. My wife proved that to be true on my thirtieth birthday. Without me knowing anything about it she invited all of my family. She chose the perfect place. She invested hours in writing invitations and making arrangements, all for me. The night of the party we drove into the parking lot, held hands as we walked to the restaurant, and all the while I thought we were only getting dinner. I loved walking into that room filled with my family and friends all shouting out to the top of their voices, "Surprise!" That moment was an amazing gift. Now that my grandma and grandpa are both in heaven, I treasure the memory of their laughter as they saw the look of surprise on my face. I loved my birthday party, but what I loved most was knowing that my wife loved me enough to do all of that for me. She may not have even realized how badly I needed that evening, but her response to my happiness warmed my heart. Her love had produced action and her action had assured me of her love. Don't allow complacency to rob you of the joy and excitement of love. Don't allow boredom to steal what should be the greatest, most fulfilling relationship in your life. Love your spouse out loud. Let the volume of your actions drown out any doubts your husband or wife may have about your love.

Stop for just a minute and think about it. When was the last time you put significant energy into showing your husband or wife how much you love him or her? When was the last time you thought of a creative way to express your feelings for your husband or wife? Too often we invest virtually no energy at all in the person we say we love most. Husband, if anyone compliments your wife more than you, that's unacceptable! Wife, if anyone admires your husband more than you, that's unacceptable! And if anyone expresses more love for either of you than you express for each other, that is a serious issue you should correct immediately.

Husband, have you ever taken the time to ask your wife what makes her feel special? Wife, have you ever asked your husband what makes him feel loved? Most often the response to these questions is no. How can it be that two people live together, see each other naked, buy houses, and have families, but they never engage in meaningful conversations about what makes them feel loved? "Understanding is a wellspring of life" (Proverbs 16:22).You need to understand your spouse in order to give life to your marriage. If you're not sure what makes your spouse feel loved how can you succeed in loving them? It's simple—you can't!

Most people are left assuming what their spouse wants, and that is incredibly dangerous because people are inherently selfish. We assume if it's great for us it must be great for them, and that usually leads to the giver being dominated by the taker. Either the husband or the wife ends up feeling like he or she is trapped under the thumb of his or her spouse. There are times and instances when that arrangement works for a while. The wife pretends to smile while she climbs on the back of the motorcycle, or she acts interested while they tour the bass pro shop. Inside she's questioning, "When was the last time we did what I wanted to do?" She watches her husband buy another toy or invest in another hobby and she says silently in her heart, "This is all he cares about." Or maybe it's the husband who feels their sexual calendar is determined by his wife. He listens while she complains about how much television he's watching or how much time he spends hunting or golfing, and inside he's thinking he has to be allowed some outlet to deal with his sexual frustration. If he said what he was really thinking it would break his wife's heart beyond repair. In counseling they would both accuse each other of being selfish, and both would be right.

People are selfish. That isn't a great revelation. We all like to have our own way. We all wish life was one big event catered in our honor. Typically we're all driven by our wants and our desires— it's part of our nature! We usually only notice selfishness in other people, and because of that it's difficult to confront how selfish **we** are. We're actually so selfish that we can even give selfishly. Jesus taught about people who give large gifts in order to be recognized (Matthew 6:2). Their gifts are a call for everyone around them to notice what's been given. For these people, it's all about special recognition, and even for those of us who would condemn such behavior it's easy to get tangled in that web. Remember, a strong desire for affirmation is embedded in all of us. We are all hardwired with selfish tendencies. Many marriages are like a continual chess match. Spouses try to use their intimate knowledge of needs and desires to strategically manipulate one another. The pursuit is ultimately the belief that your spouse exists to make you happy.

You never get angry about how little you're giving, but you're quick to point out how little you're receiving.

I'll never forget the day my wife finally helped me see that I was guilty of giving selfishly. At first my reaction was to reject her perception of my motives, and I accused her of being ridiculous. It wasn't until I stopped talking and started listening that she was able to explain the problem. There was no denying that I was trying to impress her. No condemning me for a failure to be romantically creative, but she was aware that my romantic gestures came with strings attached. I felt she didn't appreciate the creative, romantic things I was doing, but the problem wasn't her appreciation. The problem was that while I was executing my latest romantic scheme she was getting tangled up in all the strings I had attached. Her feminine intuition made her aware that my giving was being driven by expectations. She was exactly right. Like a well-choreographed dance, I had every step planned out in my mind, including how she was supposed to respond to my gift. Therefore, instead of my giving creating an atmosphere of *freedom* it actually created an atmosphere of *pressure*. That's why she was frequently unresponsive to my romantic prowess. I could have saved myself a lot of frustration if I had only listened. The brutal cycle we were caught in eventually ended after comprehension broke through my thick skull. I was able to enjoy the benefits of showing love with no strings attached. I promise things greatly improved. And I mean *greatly* improved!

Showing your spouse you love them means loving them without the inhibiting demands of selfish expectations. I'm not suggesting that one spouse be given permission to take without giving, but I am suggesting you can't give with the ulterior motive of taking. If that is occurring in your marriage you are actually not giving, but you are setting yourself up. Like a puppeteer, you attempt to pull all the right strings so you can determine the outcome, but you usually end up frustrated and furious because people are unpredictable. You're really not angry that your spouse didn't respond; you're actually frustrated that your attempts to manipulate your spouse failed. It's sad when two people get so far away from the vows they made that manipulation becomes a part of their marital routine. The husband knows how to get his wife to raise the white flag and he uses every weapon in his arsenal. The wife knows how to get her husband to say yes, how to make him the violin and herself the violinist, and too often our culture accepts this. There's a long list of jokes to prove that we do, and no less than a hundred sitcoms that portray that family dynamic as the norm. However, if the Bible is your standard, manipulation isn't acceptable, and regardless of the sitcom's story line, God isn't laughing.

Sadly, the manipulative tactics that are prevalent in our marriages come dangerously close to some form of marital prostitution." It's not, "I'm going to show you how much I love you *because* I love you," but, "I'm willing to give you what you want if you're willing to pay the price. For example, "You can have sex tonight if..." or, "I will go shopping with you if..." or, "I'll stop being so difficult if...." Surely we recognize that pattern as being detrimental to marital oneness. Not only does that kind of behavior fail to honor God, it fails to honor your marriage or your spouse. God demonstrates just the opposite by giving us His grace, and we demonstrate the opposite of God when we practice marital manipulation.

The beautiful thing about grace is that it's free. Paul in his letter to the Ephesians referred to grace as a gift (Ephesians 2:8). So the question is, how often do you perpetuate God's love by extending grace to your spouse? If you carefully examined your heart before answering that question, would you have to admit that most of your marital favors have a price tag attached? If your answer is yes, that's not true love. God shows us the way we are supposed to love others by the way He loves us. He lavishly gives us grace without limits. Grace that goes beyond the boundaries of human comprehension, and think about the enormous impact it would have on your marriage if you reflected the character of God by giving your spouse gifts of grace. Pastor and author John Piper says this in his book *This Momentary Marriage*, "Let the measure of God's grace to you in the cross of Christ be the measure of your grace to your spouse."[11] The magnitude of God's gift is immeasurable. There has never been a gift equal to Jesus, and still God gave Him graciously. The challenge presented in this phrase is enormous. Yet I pray that all of us would earnestly desire for this level of giving to prevail in our marriages.

If your question is, "How do I show my spouse I love them?" The answer is, "Only your spouse really has the answer." Clear communication is critical. You have to be able to articulate what you need and even want from your spouse. It's not wrong to have your wants fulfilled in marriage, but it *is* wrong to resent your spouse for failing to give you what you've never told him or her you want. I couldn't begin to count the times I've seen a spouse completely surprised by an admission that surfaces for the first time during a counseling session. The husband or wife asks in an elevated tone, "Why have you never told me that before?" You can tell by the look on this person's face he or she can't believe what he or she is hearing. For some odd reason married adults aren't good at equipping their spouses with the necessary information to effectively express their love. Mumbling under your breath about her isn't effective, and talking to your friends about him doesn't help anything.

Husbands and wives have to be willing to open up, and unfortunately that doesn't seem to happen often enough. Highly respected author and marriage authority Gary Smalley points out, "It is typical for a man to marry without knowing how to talk to his wife. Some men don't even know that their wives need intimate communication."[12] So why do men fail to open up? Sometimes it's because they really have no idea how to communicate. Men learn from their fathers, and an inability or an unwillingness to communicate could be an issue passed down from the previous generation. Other times, the reasons are much deeper. Some men live in fear of their wives. They hold negative feelings and emotions about their wives inside because they're afraid to tell them the truth. Most men would say, "If I tell her the truth she will make my life miserable." They would argue there's already too little sex, too much fussing, and that being open with their wives would only make things worse. Wife, if this is the vibe you're sending your husband, change. There must be open lines of communication and honesty has to be valued. A lack of communication can also be connected to depression, discouragement, or lack of self-confidence. Men may have a three-track mind—sex, food, and sleep—but often their unwillingness to communicate can be connected to complex reasons. However, silence doesn't go unheard.

Husband, what I'm trying to help you see is that your silence communicates a really loud message. It says, "I'm satisfied with what I'm receiving." *Even if your wife knows you're not satisfied, your silence gives her permission to give you more of the same.* Your wife may be a gift from God, but she can't effectively show you the love you desire if you never find the courage to express your needs. If your wife is controlling she needs to know. Or if you have a problem with the amount of time she's spending on Facebook and you need her to spend more time with you, tell her. Your silence may also be causing your wife to feel unnoticed or uninteresting. Maybe that's not even how you feel about her, but that's what she hears from your silence. She may reflect back on a time when it seemed you couldn't wait to hear the sound of her voice and wonder what's wrong with her now. When did you stop caring? Your lack of communication may also be the reason your wife frequently takes charge. She perceives your silence as indifference and she has to take the lead when she would rather have the supporting role. The point is your words and your silence both have the power to communicate, and you need to make sure it's your words that are communicating your true feelings.

Wife, in the same way you need to be open with your husband. Help him speak your love language. If he's complacent in your relationship, tell him. If more compliments or some well thought out flirtatious texts would make you feel loved, tell him. If his help around the house would make you feel more loved, let him know. You have to let him know!

The point is, showing love has to start with a conversation about the issues that assault love. It won't be an easy conversation, but it's a conversation you have to have. By talking things out, no matter what those things are, you present your spouse with an opportunity to show their love for you by attempting to meet your needs and maybe even some of your wants. I'll say more about communication in the next chapter and continue to make the case for why it has to exist in your marriage.

Maybe you're still wondering how to show your spouse you love them. If that describes how you're feeling, here is some really practical advice. We only have a few ways to express love. There are only a few tools in the chest. That means it isn't that difficult to show love when you stop and think about the limited options you have at your disposal. The Bible says, "Where your treasure is, there your heart will be also" (Matthew 6:21). Jesus teaches the things you love and value most will have the lion's share of your heart. People adore what they love. When you apply this verse to your marriage it clarifies the starting point for showing love in your marriage, and the first step is treasuring your marriage relationship. When you treasure your marriage, you will invest your heart into it. Once you're putting your whole heart into your marriage your spouse will never have to doubt whether or not he or she is loved.

Think about the ways that are available to us to express love. There are only a few, but the number one way to show love is by giving your time. That is the greatest gift you can offer your spouse. Time is our most valuable commodity. We only have a limited supply, and once it's gone, it's gone. Showing your spouse you love them enough to give him or her your most valuable commodity speaks *volumes*. There really is no substitute for time. I would also encourage those of you who say you have limited time to make the time you *do* have count.

You can also show your husband or wife you love him or her by giving him or her attention. That could be a walk in the park, a picnic, a date night, or spending quality time together. Denise and I have learned how to make a trip to the grocery store count. Even a quick lunch or an intentional evening cup of coffee together can affirm that she has my attention. I would also suggest listening. When you're listening to your husband or wife you're communicating that you value their thoughts, opinions, and requests. That's not always easy especially if you're better at talking, but practice makes perfect. The more you learn to be attentive to your spouse, the more you're showing your love for them. When you're willing to give someone your attention, you're validating them. Start practicing being attentive to your spouse. Learn to listen for the little cues that present you with an opportunity to express your love. Block out the unnecessary distractions in your life and love your husband or wife by giving them your undivided attention.

The third way we can communicate our love is through physical touch. Physical touch in a loving marriage gives tremendous confidence to both spouses. Have you ever stopped to think about the importance of physical touch? Medical science has even concluded that caring human touch is a vital contribution to the well-being of a newborn baby.[13] I would also add that caring physical touch significantly contributes to the well-being of your marriage. God gave us areas of sensitivity so those areas would respond to touch. It is important for husbands and wives to touch each other. Hold hands, caress arms, hug, kiss, and enjoy sexual intimacy together frequently. My wife and I love evenings on the couch. We talk, we show affection, and we just enjoy each other's company. It's amazing how much our intentional couch time has affected every other area of our marriage.

I would also strongly encourage every couple who reads this book to develop intimacy that doesn't involve intercourse. There will be a time in life when intercourse is no longer possible. Age, physical health, or medication can end a vibrant sexual relationship, but not if your sexual relationship involves more than intercourse. Pastor Mark Driscoll said in his best-selling book, "A devoted friend is dependable through varying seasons of life."[14] The couple who enjoys a friendship can remain lovers and enjoy intimacy through every season of their marriage. Neither age nor time has the power to diminish true friendship.

In addition to all of the ways we've already discussed, you can also practice generosity or creativity. The spouse who invests thought and time into creatively expressing love definitely collects a return on their investment. I learned that valuable lesson not long after Denise and I were married. We were living in a small, mobile home in the foothills of North Carolina. We had no money at all. We were so poor we had to buy hats to wear when looking out the window so the neighbors would think we had clothes on. Our indoor furniture was actually outdoor furniture, and when it rained we had to lay towels under the windows because so much water leaked in. To add insult to injury, the place was so old I tried to paint it with a brush and brown latex paint. It didn't take me long to realize that wasn't a good idea, but at the time it was the best I could do.

A few months after our wedding we were going to share our first Valentine's Day as husband and wife. I can still remember worrying about what I was going to do for the love of my life. She deserved diamonds but they weren't an option. My desperation motivated me to be creative. Valentine's Day arrived and my wife walked into our kitchen. There were three roses in a vase serving as a centerpiece on our outdoor table. I had cooked the best Italian dinner I possibly could, and hanging from our ceiling were red hearts I had cut from construction paper and attached to red yarn. They were hanging all through the house, and each heart had a personal message that described my love for the woman who had made my dreams come true. That night it didn't matter that we didn't have any money, and it didn't matter that we were in our small mobile home. Creativity allowed me to express my love without an expensive gift or an elaborate evening on the town.

My advice is, don't underestimate the impact of a simple gift. It doesn't have to be a Bentley or a sprawling estate to say "I love you." Sometimes it's just dropping by the store to pick up your husband or wife's favorite sweet treat. I love the look on my wife's face when I walk through the door with a dark chocolate Snickers candy bar, and she loves the look on my face when she wakes me up to fresh biscuits baking in the oven. I know these aren't expensive gifts, but they're just simple ways to say "I was thinking about you today." You don't always have to spend money—just be willing to spend yourself. The most important word in a marriage relationship is "effort." How much effort you're willing to give to your marriage communicates how much you value your marriage. Andy Stanley, Pastor of North Point Community Church, once said at a conference, "I can't promise that I will fill your cup completely up, but I can promise I will pour mine completely out." Are you willing to say that to your husband or wife? Are you willing to practice that in your marriage?

In the last chapter I'll be saying a lot more about effort, but for right now you need to show your spouse you love them. Please take a moment, think about it, and then decide how you're going to do that.

CHAPTER 4:
Love is Serious

Your relationship with Jesus is the most important relationship in your life. As a matter of fact, that relationship impacts every area of your life and every moment of your eternity. Without that relationship, nothing else really matters. Any work you dedicate to your marriage suddenly becomes meaningless if you don't have a personal relationship with Jesus.

Second only to your relationship with Jesus is your relationship with your spouse. That's why it is paramount that your marriage relationship be seen as a priority. I can't emphasize enough how important it is for your marriage to be healthy. If it is not, every other aspect of your life will suffer. You can only fake it for so long. Eventually the wear and tear of your secret struggle overwhelms you. Your life is—and will be—powerfully influenced by the quality of your marriage. People who are trapped in the purgatory of a miserable marriage carry the effects of the damage into every facet of their lives. I'm not talking about isolated areas of life, but I'm talking about *every* area of life. That means your public life, private life, parental life, and even your spiritual life. All of these areas are impacted by the quality of your marriage relationship. That is why love is serious.

The love between a husband and wife is so serious that God has promised everyone who violates that love will be prosecuted (Hebrews 13:4). Our culture's whimsical attitude toward marriage doesn't reflect God's attitude at all—when it comes to marriage, God couldn't be more serious! Knowing that should intensify our respect of this great commitment called marriage. I usually urge couples to think about the enormous weight of the marriage vows. Just before they speak those words during the wedding ceremony I usually say to them, "Outside of your prayer for salvation these will be the most important words of your lives." I've never had a couple stop me at that moment and say, "I can't make those promises." They always smile as they clasp each other's hands and repeat every phrase after me. But sadly, people allow the river of time to pull them farther and farther away from the seriousness of those words. The storms of life or the pain of neglect cause them to forget "till death do us part."

Oh sure, I believe love can be fun and adventurous. I believe love can be exhilarating and satisfying, but above everything else love has to be taken *seriously*. I realize that statement flies directly in the face of current pop culture. Most people now have the idea that love is little more than a word. We've become adolescent regarding love. We're like preteens throwing around the word without even realizing what it really means. But God knows what it means. He knew before He created people that His love for them would one day require Him to give His Son to demonstrate that love. For those of you who have wrestled with the question, "Why did God offer His Son's life," you now know the answer: it was all because of love. So if you consult God, you realize that to Him love looks like Calvary. To Him love looks like a cross. It looks like Jesus hanging with arms spread wide open as if to say, "I love you this much." To God, love looks like His Son becoming the recipient of the sins of the whole world. That's why love is serious to God, and that's why it should be serious to us.

Love issues a call to an extreme place. It forcefully beckons us to make the unfamiliar a familiar life's practice. Love requires us to practice valuing someone else's life more than our own. It requires us to gladly surrender our life to being inseparably intertwined with someone else's life. Love calls us to a place of relational safety where no weapon can penetrate the heart of our marriage. That's why love has to be taken seriously—true love was created by God for our protection. True love protects us from sin. Like a shield, it guards us from extramarital sexual or emotional relationships. Virtually every week I receive word that another husband or wife has strayed. It's overwhelming to stop and think about the huge number of affairs that take place in the small part of the world that surrounds us. People reaching for something they believe will be more fulfilling. Men and women risking everything they've worked for in an attempt to fill a void that exists in their lives. Often they become the targets of harsh criticism and judgment. People take aim and fire cruel accusations at them, and then in the same breath they're quick to offer their diagnosis of what went wrong. The conversation usually revolves around the dirtiest of the details as the person lured away by sin gets dragged through the mud. Rarely do people focus on the unseen problem that was well hidden behind closed doors:

No one seems to notice when a husband or wife stops pursuing the heart of God.

No one sees prayerlessness or recognizes when a person's love for God is growing cold. But there's always a moment when intensity is replaced by contentment and a close walk with God grows distant. However, while it is impossible for people to be aware of that moment, the enemy is well aware of that moment. He sees his opportunity to wreak havoc in the life of the person whose heart is cold on God and he always seizes that opportunity. Satan is certainly a lot of negative things, but "ignorant" isn't one of them. He knows when a person is out of balance it's really easy for them to be swayed to the point of falling. He always unleashes his attack at just the right moment.

Christians rarely notice their lives being out of focus and seldom feel the foundation of their faith shifting. It's usually so gradual. The journey from right to wrong is made by taking one step at a time. You feel the coldness between you and Jesus for a moment, but then you get acclimated and you're ready to take the next step. Sadly, once a close relationship with God falters, *sin follows*. An unnoticed step in the wrong direction eventually leads to a life wrecked by sin, and too often marriages are destroyed by what once seemed innocent. That's why it is so important that your love for your spouse be connected to your love for God. Loving God with all your heart creates a deeper love for your spouse. Loving God with all your heart will protect you from straying from your spouse. Loving God with all your heart will heighten your commitment to purity and will strengthen the foundation of your marriage. Being fully dedicated to God teaches you to be more dedicated to your spouse. That intentional stare or flirtatious smile, that conversation in the break room or that message on Facebook will be less likely to occur in a marriage saturated by true love.

Your marital goal has to be *true* love. You have to be serious about that! Never assume that an affair could never happen to you.

James MacDonald, founder of Harvest Bible Chapel and acclaimed author, wisely says, "It is impossible for us to dwell on desire for any length of time without rationalizing a way to get it by making the particular sin more attractive and accessible than it really is. When we dwell on desire, yielding is only a matter of time."[15] If you entertain the idea you will eventually be engaging in the reality. I say often, "Never look to an outside source to meet a marital need." Never assume you securely hold the heart of your spouse. Never assume you live beyond the possibility of divorce. Never ignore your need to continually strengthen your walk with God. Never stop aggressively pursuing the heart of your husband or wife. Even the most beautiful gardens require constant attention, and the more they are groomed the more beauty they reveal.

Sometimes marriage isn't very pleasant. Dennis and Barbara Rainey admit, "Like the jarring, repetitive beep of an alarm clock, the shocking jolt of disappointment eventually affects all couples."[16] The truth is, living with someone isn't easy, and at times marriage can be painful. Unfortunately, we are all prone to hurt those we love. A bad day at work leads to a bad evening at home, an exhausting day with the kids initiates a fiery argument, or a simple misunderstanding leads to a harsh confrontation. Every married couple has lived through these moments. Your spouse is inevitably going to do something that crosses the line. Your patience will be tested and your boundaries will be stretched beyond their limit. Those moments are destined to be a part of every marriage, but they shouldn't mark the end of a marriage. You actually have to make a choice regarding how you are going to respond. You can act like a pressure cooker and blow off a lot of steam, or you can act like a brain donor and give your spouse a piece of your mind. While both of these responses are wrong, at least they're not long-term. Unfortunately, that isn't the case with the person who responds to conflict by acting like a filing cabinet. He or she records the offense and files the hurt away to reach for it again in the future. Max Lucado says in his book, *In the Grip of Grace*:

Call it a bad addiction. We start the habit innocently enough, indulging our hurts with doses of anger. Not much, just a needle or two of rancor. The rush numbs the hurt, so we come back for more and up the dosage .... Drugged on malice, the roles are reversed; we aren't the victim, we're the victor.[17]

People who handle conflict like a filing cabinet store their anger away and each time they revisit the pain their anger festers. They completely ignore the fact the Bible says that love keeps no record when it is wronged (1 Corinthians 13:5). Over and over again they quietly hide their pain until all their files are full. Once they reach that point there should be a warning label plastered on them that reads, "Contents Under Pressure," or "Impending Explosion." Eventually the wrong word is spoken or an offense is committed and the explosion occurs. When that happens, a marriage's only hope of avoiding long-term damage is true love. When we're angry we instantly recall all of the negative things our spouse has ever done, and if we talk while we're angry we'll always say things that shouldn't be said. Once those violent words are spoken, there is no taking them back. Those moments can be extremely hurtful and even damaging. Cheryl Scruggs testifies to this fact as she recounts her affair in the book, *I Am Second*:

> We got married thinking we could complete each other, that we somehow could make each other whole. But I wasn't whole. I felt empty. I was missing something. I got it in my head that it was Jeff's fault, that he wasn't meeting my needs. I got angry because Jeff couldn't understand my pain. The

more time passed, the angrier I got. I never showed
it, but on the inside I was emotionally divorcing
him, cutting him out of my life.[18]

True love protects us from harboring resentment against our
spouse, and without it marriage becomes a distant place. Mark and
Grace Driscoll share in the book they co-authored, "Forgiveness is
not dying emotionally and no longer feeling the pain of transgres-
sion. Rather, forgiveness allows us to feel the appropriate depth of
grievous pain but choose by grace not to be continually paralyzed
or defined by it."[19] Forgiving your spouse doesn't mean you allow
yourself to be trampled on, but it does mean you turn the other
cheek. That's not the demand of your spouse, but the demand of
Jesus (Luke 6:29). True love reminds us that our relationship with
God is based on forgiveness, and that God's love for us ultimately
protects us from His wrath (Romans 5:8–9). Conviction rises from
that awareness, and God's light shines into the dark crevices of our
hearts.

When true love is at work in your marriage it operates like
a security system, sounding an alarm at the first detection of an
intruder. True love leads you to become more sensitive to your
spouse's feelings, and that sensitivity is a strong deterrent to emotional assaults. If you truly love your spouse, you would never want
to break their heart. Think about it; you would never intentionally
hurt someone you love. Even as you work through painful situa-
tions you do so with tenderness. Your ultimate hope should always
be healing. Love instinctively leads us to protect. When you're
serious about love, you're serious about guarding the heart of the
one you love. Sin in marriage doesn't always occur because of the
presence of the devil, but it often occurs because of the *absence* of
true godly love. It is vitally important that you work to make sure

your marriage is based on true love. That serious approach to loving your spouse will give way to a marriage you can count on. True love never flees, it only clings, and if your marriage is held together by true love, it will stand the test of time. Your marriage will endure regardless of how severe the storm might be, or how bad the trial may seem. If two people are seriously in love they will always be drawn closer together, never farther apart.

Effort is Serious

The effort you invest in your marriage communicates how much you value your marriage. The harder you work to make sure your spouse is fulfilled, the more you reveal your love for them. Everyone loves flattery. Someone saying all the right things can be powerfully persuasive, but flattery creates infatuation, and you're interested in something much deeper than that. The reason you're taking the time to read this book is because you're interested in real love. Forget puppy love or fair-weather love, you're interested in real, lasting love. That is the love that most satisfies the longing inside us, but that level of love requires extreme effort.

One of the worst statements ever made regarding marriage is that it has to be fifty-fifty. This statement describes a husband giving fifty percent of his energy equally matched by a wife giving fifty percent of her energy. In reality that means neither is giving their all, and that's a recipe for failure. Marriage requires a husband to give one hundred percent to his wife and a wife to give one hundred percent to her husband. It's not a two-way street, but it's a one-way street with both people traveling in the same direction. You have to roll up your sleeves and go to work if you want your marriage to be successful. Jim George said in *A Man After God's Own Heart*, "Intimacy possesses multiple facets and is multi-layered. It is hard work."[20] There are no quick fixes or immediate solutions, but a satisfying marriage is the result of consistent effort.

On our wedding day I looked into my wife's beautiful hazel eyes and I promised to create a home where she would be loved and cared for. With that promise I declared my acceptance of *all* of her needs. Any baggage she had, any residual pain from past hurts, any insecurities or expectations all became mine as I vowed to give my life to her. That's what marriage is: vowing to give everything you have and everything you are through every season of life. Marriage is a husband saying to his wife, "I am yours," and a wife saying to her husband, "I am yours." "My devotion is yours, my body is yours, my future is yours, and my love is yours." Marriage is a man and a woman willingly accepting each other's needs and desires, two people answering a higher calling to live beyond themselves. Effort ultimately emerges from the fertile ground of a true commitment to marital oneness.

True marital oneness means you love your spouse as much as you love yourself (Ephesians 5:28–29). You work for your spouse's satisfaction as much as you work for your own satisfaction. You work for your spouse's fulfillment as much as you work for your own fulfillment. Marital oneness is looking in the mirror and seeing your spouse's reflection because *you are one.* I understand if you feel challenged by this view of marriage. I also realize this view is much deeper than the shallow practice of a quick wedding leading to a long party that we often see in our culture. You should also realize that reaching this depth of marital oneness doesn't happen in a day or a year, but it happens as you *daily* live out your commitment to your spouse.

Denise and I lived several years of our marriage without realizing how to honor each other. We were married before our twentieth birthdays and were very ignorant about what to expect. We really had no idea how to be married, and sadly, no one ever really told us. It was even more difficult because we were in public ministry while privately being in pain. It wasn't that we didn't love each other—we simply didn't know how to work through our problems. We were two kids with lots of adult responsibilities and no well of experience to draw from. We realized after our marriage that we both had different expectations of what marriage would be like, and it wasn't what either of us thought it would be. The only thing that helped us survive those years was our commitment to a life-long marriage.

We both believed in the words "till death do us part." Divorce was never an option, and living together without that option was our incentive to make our marriage better. Thankfully, that's exactly what happened: *better.* I understand now that storms never last forever. Our season of ignorance and emptiness was only temporary. I understand that storms seem as if they will last forever, but I also understand the importance of looking beyond the moment and honoring your commitment to your marriage. Storms never last forever! Denise often says, "Even when marriage isn't good, it's still a commitment." Marital oneness is possible, but you have to overcome all its enemies to experience its rewards. When you're living through a moment that feels like its tearing you apart, reach for something that will hold you together. Denise and I are a living testimony of the joys that exists after the tears. Marital oneness is worth it!

Several years ago I learned a great lesson in marital effort by watching my father-in-law care for my mother-in-law during her seven-year battle with cancer. Their marriage had survived the hardships they encountered in their early years and had blossomed into a beautiful example of love and friendship. They had reached the place that even their disagreements were cute. The whole family would joke with both of them about their unwillingness to be wrong, but that didn't matter because time had endeared them to each other. Their little spats would usually end with her saying (with a slight growl), "John ...." and he would respond, "All right, Mama." The love they felt for each other as high school sweethearts had been tested but it hadn't failed. Their lives were a great example of God *first* and family *second*, which is the correct order. Christmas was a grand event, but no more special than weekly Sunday lunches with everyone around the table. Rachel would cook and John would pray.

The family was always together, even when we received the news that Rachel had a malignant tumor. I still remember seeing John fall to his knees the moment the doctor shared the devastating news. I will never forget the doctor's words: "Some tumors are benign, but unfortunately this one is not." That moment was dominated by questions: "What does this mean?", "Where do we go from here?", "How long does she have to live?" They were only in their early forties, and this wasn't supposed to be happening. They had just celebrated the birth of their granddaughter. They also had plans to experience new places and things together. Unfortunately, all of that seemed to disappear as life proved its point again: the only thing that is certain is uncertainty, and the only thing we can expect is the unexpected.

However, it was during that season of tears and pain that John proved how willing he was to gift Rachel with effort. He became a nurse, a caregiver, an encourager, a maid, and a cook while maintaining his role as a husband. Cancer changed so much in their lives, but it never once changed the fact they were best friends. He lovingly sat by her bed during repeated hospital stays. He was so committed to being with her that he typically refused to go home for extra clothes. If anyone was going to be there with her, it was going to be him. Each time she called his name he answered— regardless of how tired he was. Eventually cancer took away her strength but revealed John's willingness to care for her without limits. Rachel had always been strong, but now during her season of weakness it was John who held her hand as she struggled to walk on her own. Nightly he slept by her hospital bed just in case she needed his help. It was more difficult than ordering roses or planning a night out on the town, but it was an expression of the depth of his commitment. All of it was being done in secret for her eyes only, and it loudly communicated to her that she was loved. It was *John* who was by her side the morning angels escorted her into the presence of the only One who loved her more than *he* did. Looking back now I realize it was John's close relationship with God that gave him the strength to tirelessly love his wife, and that love produced true effort.

None of us know what we will go through. We *do* know eventually life will deal us an overwhelming blow, and eventually one of us will walk in John's shoes. That is why it's important that you know your spouse is serious about effort, that you view giving to your spouse *now* as a dress rehearsal for the *future*. Marriage isn't always "for better and for richer." It isn't always going to be "in health," but eventually there will be "for worse," "for poorer," and "in sickness." The love your spouse has for you isn't proven during an exciting sexual experience or a romantic vacation, but it's proven when they give knowing you can't give in return. Those moments do require effort, but those moments are a beautiful demonstration of why God created marriage.

Effort is driven by the desire to satisfy your spouse, the desire to experience the blessing that occurs when you esteem your spouse above yourself. John the Baptist received the greatest compliment ever uttered by Jesus because he lived as an example of humility. His willingness to decrease so that Jesus could increase earned him the right to be called the greatest man born of a woman (Matthew 11:11). The more John abased himself the more he subsequently exalted Jesus. Anytime we demote ourselves we create an opportunity to promote someone else. This is proven true in our relationship with Jesus and in our relationship with our spouse. You can't lift your spouse onto a pedestal if you are above him or her. True love never stands on a pedestal attempting to pull someone else up, but true love finds contentment in bowing down in order to raise someone else up. This won't be easy because self-deprivation is never easy. However, you know effort is occurring in your marriage when your heartfelt desire is to elevate your spouse to a position of greater significance. Effort is occurring when your love for your spouse is so generous it's clearly visible through your actions. According to Jim George, "True biblical love is a selfless commitment of one's body, soul, and spirit to the betterment of the other person."[21] This will only happen when you genuinely see your husband or wife's needs as important. As long as you think the things that matter to them *don't* matter, then true effort will be nonexistent.

Sadly, a marriage without effort also becomes nonexistent.

Needs that are carelessly disregarded by an indifferent spouse eventually become serious points of contention. Conversations become arguments as you try to communicate what's missing in your marriage. You eventually start asking yourself if your husband or wife could act this way and really be in love with you. You're married, you have the ring to prove it, yet you feel completely abandoned. There seems to be this gaping hole inside of you that remains empty while your spouse ignores all your attempts to attract his or her attention.

All of this happens because unmet needs never simply disappear; they only become more intense. Eventually you reach the place where your unmet need dominates your thoughts. Your mind starts creating schemes and devising plans that will lead to your fulfillment. Eventually you find yourself searching for ways to have your unmet need fulfilled—regardless of the aftermath. If your unmet need is sexual, you turn to Internet pornography or you strongly communicate your availability to someone who's willing to meet your sexual needs. If your unmet need is emotional, you find yourself in a chat room or on Facebook or even cultivating an emotional affair. All too often people are blind to sin they're yielding to, as they're being driven by their unmet needs. That's why unmet needs are extremely dangerous. By design we all have needs, and our needs are as much a part of who we are as our strengths. You can't find anyone who doesn't have needs, but you can find plenty of people who lose sight of reality when they're controlled by their needs. The greener grass on the other side of the fence has to be mowed just as often as the grass you already have. There is no perfect person who exists to meet your needs without ever requiring you to meet his or her needs as well.

Sex is Serious

God created us with needs. He created us knowing we would crave having our needs met. Thankfully, He also created marriage and designed men and women with the ability to meet one another's needs. God's design of the male and female body proves His interest in our pleasure. He even designed the female clitoris exclusively for sexual pleasure. It was God who designed a man's body to experience total elation during ejaculation. Sex is one of God's great creations. He designed us to desire sex. That desire is good, right, and even godly as long as it is reserved for marriage.

United States Olympian track star Lolo Jones shared in an interview with Bryant Gumbel that she is saving herself sexually until she's married. She said, "It's the hardest thing I've ever done in my life, harder than training for the Olympics. Harder than studying for college has been staying a virgin before marriage."[22] The reason it's so hard to wait is because we desire sex. Hormones are released in our bodies, creating an intense craving to experience sexual intercourse. God doesn't want to keep sex from us, but He does want us to wait until we're married.

Once you're married there are no limitations on how much sex you can enjoy except the limitations you create. Marriage gives us permission to experience each other's bodies sexually with God's blessing (Hebrews 13:4). The Bible presents marriage as a deterrent to committing sexual sin. Scripture clearly addresses our lack of sexual self-control and calls husbands —as well as wives — to gift one another with sexual satisfaction (1 Corinthians 7). By God's design a satisfying sexual relationship brings you closer together and also strengthens your chances of maintaining marital purity. A husband or wife who repeatedly says no or half-heartedly says yes places his or her spouse at risk. Also, a husband or wife who fails to satisfy their spouse risks jeopardizing the success of their marriage. Author Kevin Leman wrote in his best-selling book, *Sheet Music,* "But if you're married, sex will be one of the most important parts of your life, whether you want it to be that way or not. If you don't treat sex this way—as a matter of extreme importance—you're shortchanging yourself, your spouse and your kids."[23]

Sex is extremely important! A satisfying sex life isn't everything, but it is a strong contributor to a happy marriage. By treating sex as important you communicate that your spouse's satisfaction is important—and not just important in general, but important to you. If sex is important, you won't give it with an attitude, but with a mutual desire to please each other. Sex teaches us to value our spouse's satisfaction. We have sex because we want to satisfy and to be satisfied.

Unfortunately, a lot of married people would describe their sex lives as unsatisfying. Countless women struggle with sexual desire because they rarely achieve orgasm, but they never find the strength to tell their husbands. The wife who doesn't tell her husband causes him to live with the pain of feeling undesirable and unwanted. He needs to know the truth. How can he succeed in satisfying his wife if she never takes the time to equip him with the knowledge he needs to satisfy her? She is secretly robbing him of the necessary information he needs to fulfill her sexually. Most husbands strongly desire to satisfy their wives completely. The majority of men I've counseled say their greatest sexual reward is sexually pleasing their wives. They feel empowered when their wives audibly and physically respond during intercourse. One primary reason that is true is because a man's masculinity is typically connected to how well he performs sexually. By withholding information from her husband, the wife jeopardizes them enjoying a fulfilling sexual relationship. She also prevents her husband from learning how to satisfy her.

Wives, please don't allow your marriage bed to be violated because of a lie. Allow your husband to show his love for you sexually by listening to your wants and your instructions, and then proving to you that your satisfaction matters to him. There is nothing ungodly or wrong about showing your husband how to help you achieve an orgasm. Dr. Kevin Leman, in his book *Sheet Music,* recommends, "Get to know yourself well enough that you can help your husband learn what makes you heat up … you've got some exploring to do—you've got to learn what makes you tick."[24] Once you learn what makes you tick you have the opportunity to teach your husband what lights your fire. For some of you this might sound intimidating, but it *can* be exciting. I don't know a husband who wouldn't find it extremely erotic and sexually arousing to feel his wife's hot breath against his ear, whispering her intimate desires, and guiding him to her amazing moment. There is nothing wrong with openly expressing what you long to experience in bed. Throughout the Song of Solomon sex between Solomon and his bride was extremely verbal. Kisses, caresses and sexual desires were requested with exquisite detail. Learning the power of sexual communication could lead to a newfound passion in your marriage bed, but that level of intimacy requires overcoming your inhibitions about sex. Adam and Eve began their lives together naked and unashamed (Genesis 2:25). There is no shame in baring everything as you carefully equip your husband with the intimate knowledge of your body.

I would also encourage every husband to tell your wife how she can fulfill your desires. I have personally counseled men who express their desire to be true to their wives, but in the same breath confess their struggle with boredom. An older man said to me one day, "I have had the missionary position for so long it's even affected the way I feel about missions." Christian men desire uninhibited sex and that is not a sinful desire. *Lifelessness in the bedroom doesn't equal godliness.* There is nothing wrong with excitement. Your bedroom shouldn't be boring!

Let your fountain be blessed, and rejoice in the wife of your youth, a lovely deer, a graceful doe. Let her breast satisfy you at all times with delight; be enraptured [intoxicated] with her love (Proverbs 5:18–19).

Rejoicing with your wife, being satisfied by her breast, and being intoxicated with her love doesn't sound boring to me. When you read the Song of Solomon (which God inspired), it's obvious that sex between a husband and wife should be erotic. Seduction and passion are not unreasonable expectations. Solomon and his bride enjoyed things that many Christians would consider off-limits. Their sexual interaction was verbal, it was sensual, and it was satisfying. Sex feels good because God designed it to feel good. Monogamy shouldn't be a prison, but a place of protection, permission, and pleasure.

The great lesson in the Song of Solomon is the importance of maintaining passion in your marriage. Once Solomon's Shulamite wife made excuses to avoid intimacy, it didn't take long for their passionate marriage to fail (Song of Solomon chapter 5). Abstinence is supposed to be practiced outside of marriage, but not inside of marriage. It is no accident that Christian couples frequently struggle with sexual issues. Satan is like a roaring lion that's searching out people to devour (1 Peter 5:8). Spouses who are angry and empty because they're sexually deprived are far more susceptible to moral failure. Make sure your spouse isn't vulnerable to Satan's attack because you've excused yourself from sexual intimacy. Satan has many angles available to him in our culture, and marital apathy only provides him with one more. Dr. Gary and Barbara Rosberg, award-winning authors and founders of the international ministry, America's Family Coaches, wrote, "Remember your husband is a sexual being. Honor your husband by taking seriously his need for sex with you. Consider it a joy and privilege to be the one God has chosen to satisfy those needs." This statement was directed to wives, but it's equally important for husbands. It is completely wrong for a spouse to have to beg for sex. Are you so selfish that you're willing to punish your spouse for being faithful? Do you want them to look to an outside source to meet a marital need? Far too often the sins that destroy marriages are complacency and unavailability.

I realize there are times when health, physical tiredness, or life's stress makes sexual intimacy difficult, but saying no should be uncommon. Pushing your husband or wife away literally *pushes them away*. Sex is a powerful craving and marriage is intended to satisfy that appetite (1 Corinthians 7:9). Husband, each time your wife makes herself available to you she's vulnerable, so be careful how you respond. Wife, each time your husband makes himself available to you, you have the opportunity to empower him or emasculate him. Sex isn't the solution to every problem, but a healthy sex life will help you avoid a lot of potential problems. It will connect you, diminish anxiety, and make you more appreciative of each other. Through detailed conversations, uninhibited openness, great awareness, and careful exploration, you can have an incredible sex life. But you will never have real sexual fulfillment without consistent effort. There will be those electric moments when both husband and wife connect with intensity and passion while fireworks boom in the background (thank God for those times), but there will also be those moments when you selflessly satisfy your spouse as an expression of sacrificial love. The key to a satisfying sex life isn't how erotic you're willing to be, but how much effort you're willing to give. Sex is serious.

Communication is serious

The success of your marriage will not be determined by the passion in your bedroom, but by the strength of your communication. Being lovers is vitally important, but being friends is essential. You can't have a successful marriage without friendship, and you can't have a close friendship without communication. Intimate, open conversations reveal who you really are. It is through ongoing conversation that you discover a person's character, preferences, and desires. The Bible says it's out of the abundance of the heart that the mouth speaks (Matthew 12:34). There's no need to consult with a marriage counselor about the importance of communication. The authority of the Bible assures you that your words reveal who you really are. That's information your spouse has to have in order to intimately know you.

No one should ever be more informed about your life than your spouse. He or she has to know more about you than your parents, your siblings, or your friends do. Information about your hurts, your confusions, and even your celebrations should always reach them first. This has to be a matter of conviction in your marriage. If that conviction doesn't currently exist in your marital relationship, I strongly recommend that you implement it immediately. Make positively sure that open communication is one of the foundational principles of your marriage. That has to be a non-negotiable!

Dennis and Barbara Rainey, hosts of FamilyLife and respected authors, said in their book *Staying Close*, "Unless you lovingly and energetically nurture and maintain your marriage, you will begin to drift apart from your mate."[25] Drifting apart is opposite of God's desire for your marriage. He desires us to grow more intimately connected. Your conversations should be so open and intimate that they reveal uncommon knowledge. As husband and wife you should have your own vault of classified information reserved for your ears only: inside jokes, nuances, and physical gestures that signal to your spouse what you're thinking. Like Indian smoke signals, your communication should be so well tuned that you can reveal your thoughts without saying a word. It's called chemistry, and that closeness will develop over time if you maintain strong marital communication. Reaching that level of communication ensures that you're more intimate, more aligned, and more deeply connected with each other. The great thing is you *can* have this in your marriage. It's not unattainable. The first step is honestly assessing where you are and talking about where you want to be. It starts with communicating.

Instead, what often happens in marriage is a migration toward becoming silent partners. People spend years together only to find themselves living with a stranger. Marriages seem to be successful to everyone on the outside, but behind closed doors two people are trapped in a lifeless relationship. They never have or maybe never will pursue divorce, but secretly they're victims of marital separation. They're best described as two people living under the same roof, but worlds apart. Over time, the people who are trapped in these lifeless marriages learn to invest in similar things. They need some reason to be married. You'll usually hear them make statements like "We're staying together for the children," or "It's better for us financially if we stay together." Their reasoning is flawed and their oneness is artificial. They share a mortgage, a family, and often a faith but they lack true intimacy. Cohabitating is much easier for them when life is busy. As long as they're busy with work, chasing the kids, or preoccupied with intentional distractions they can co-exist without it being too obvious. However, the day finally comes when the kids are gone. Instead of a table for four they're sitting at a table for two. Instead of running through the house chasing the kids, they're sitting in a quiet living room alone. The noise that once drowned out their silence has disappeared, and emptiness of their relationship becomes a haunting reality.

If you're thinking this is some rare occurrence, you couldn't be more wrong. The scenario I've just described isn't a minimal statistic, but a common reality. John Gottman, known for his work on marital stability, and director of The Relationship Research Institute considers *withdrawal* as one of the leading causes of divorce.[26] Over time people become the victims of an undercurrent that pulls them deeper and deeper into solitude.

A few years ago my wife and I were eating at one of our favorite restaurants. Our hearts were broken as we watched an elderly couple miserably endure each other's company while eating dinner. I'm sure you've noticed the same situation; a husband and wife sitting alone at a table together—inches apart but completely isolated. That's exactly what we observed that night. The husband never acknowledged his wife, and the wife reciprocated his lack of interest. They didn't speak one single word, and not one smile was exchanged. They had tolerated the coldness in their relationship for so long they had learned to live without closeness or communication. It was literally as if both of them had their own world. The border between them seemed heavily guarded and impenetrable. They managed to create distance between themselves in spite of sitting close enough to hold hands. They were so nonexistent to each other that they could canvas the room without once allowing their eyes to meet. It was sad to think that neither one of them had many years left, yet they still failed to appreciate that moment together. As we looked across the restaurant from our table to theirs we saw clearly what we never want to become. I never want my relationship with Denise to be distant. I pray we always enjoy and appreciate each other's company. I never want to get to the point that I'm no longer intrigued by her thoughts, ideas, and conversations.

The moment you no longer have meaningful conversations is the moment you no longer have an intimate connection. Communication is the gateway to understanding the heart of your spouse. It takes you beyond the superficial. It allows you to experience true friendship. Communicating your heart allows you and your spouse to unify your thoughts, dreams, concerns, and passions. Just as prayer deepens your relationship with God, intimate communication gives depth and substance to your marriage. Too often people have the idea that marriage is about the bedroom or the bank account when in fact strong marriages are really about great communication. However, the reason so many couples never experience the connection that is created through communication is because they fail to invest the time required. Cultivating great communication in your marriage is like growing a garden; it requires time and patience. Meaningful conversations don't happen in moments. Ultimately you prove your commitment to communication by the way you appropriate your time. If you fail to create time to talk, you will fail to talk. Those of you who are already thinking, "But I don't have time …" need to make time. Most people already have more to do than a twenty-four hour day allows, but if we're honest we still manage to do the things that really matter to us.

When your marriage matters it calls you to schedule your life differently. Make sure your schedule proves to your spouse that spending time with them matters. For some of you this might be really difficult because of your work schedule or your busy lives as parents. We all have obligations that make life difficult by limiting our time. But limited time doesn't mean you can't have quality time. You have to learn to make sure the time you have counts. Moments matter! And it doesn't matter how busy you are, I believe everyone can create moments. A great question to ask yourselves would be, "How often do we work together to create moments?" or, "How committed are we to making sure there is time for us?" If your honest answer is, "Not enough," then you need to commit to creating more time for your marriage. Learn the value of working together. Men shouldn't be too cool to wash dishes or fold towels if it means more time with their wives. Women shouldn't work till bedtime on things that can wait until later. Two people can conquer time-consuming tasks better than one. Two people putting children to bed, two people washing dishes, two people cleaning the house always creates more time for two people to spend together. No matter what it costs or how much it requires, you have to make sure you have time together. There is no substitute for *together*! God didn't create marriage so you could have a wedding. He created marriage so you could be together, and you should fight anything in life that pulls you apart.

The moments Denise and I create for each other are precious. They connect us, they reinforce us, and they glue us together. Those moments remind me of all of the reasons I fell in love with her. She's not the house cleaner, clothes washer, hygienist, or mother in those moments, instead she's my sweetheart. I love those moments. I love them so much that I'm willing to be house cleaner, clothes washer, towel folder, or vacuum operator. Time with her means that much *because she's worth it*! I cherish those moments. They are priceless. However, those moments have to be created, and when they are, they deserve to be cherished. Husband, make sure your wife knows she is cherished by creating time to communicate with her, time when your attention is focused solely on her. She is the final moment in the Super Bowl, the last lap of the Daytona 500, the last round of the main event, the final inning of the World Series. Intentionally give more attention to the sound of her voice than the sound of the television, look up from your laptop or turn off the iPad. Allow her voice to take precedence over every meaningless distraction. That's the gift she wants you to give her.

Recently I took my wife on a date to her favorite restaurant. As we pulled into the parking space I placed my cell phone in the console and took her by the hand. We went inside and enjoyed an incredible meal together without my typical vice taking my attention away from her. I didn't realize she even noticed until we left and she softly said thank you. I responded by asking, "Thank you for what?" And she said, "For leaving your cell phone in the car and having an uninterrupted evening with me." I couldn't help but think how unbelievable it was that this beautiful woman who's been by my side for all these years still wants my attention. She wants me to hear her. She wants her voice to captivate my attention, and that's something men too often ignore.

Husband, you show appreciation for your wife when you practice listening to her conversations. You demonstrate how valuable she is to you when you give her your undivided attention. This assures your wife and validates your love for her. Public affection will never win her heart as much as private conversations. She knows she matters to you when her thoughts matter to you. When you're willing to be unselfish and sacrifice what's urgent *to you* for what's urgent *to her*. I know men usually think the details don't matter—the fact the dress had been marked down twice and she found it in the most unlikely place seems pointless, for example—but she loves the details! She wants you to respond to her, and since I'm talking to men I should make it clear that grunts and noises aren't real responses. An occasional "uh-huh" or "uh-uh" doesn't qualify as meaningful conversation. Husband, love your wife enough to listen to her and be engaged by her. The more you listen to her the more you will know her, and the more you know her the better you will be able to satisfy her needs. Communication opens the door to your wife's heart.

Wife, you should also practice communicating with your husband. Learn to speak his language. Realize that your communicating with him is much different than his communicating with you. You want attention to details and he wants detailed attention. Give him confidence and assurance by valuing his needs. Learn to show your appreciation for him. Be sure you frequently affirm him. Appeal that part of his nature that craves your affirmation. You'll have the prettiest yard in your neighborhood if you convince your husband that he looks hot riding the lawn mower. Tell him his muscles look sexy when he's pushing the vacuum. Sell him on that idea a couple of times; make him believe it and he'll keep the floor spotless. He responds to affirmation because he's hardwired with the desire to be affirmed. The majority of men *love* affirmation. His neurons experience hyperactivity when you compliment him. He knows when your hands are holding his arm as you walk through a crowd. It makes him feel like "the man" for that moment. He knows he's not "the man" in the world's eyes; he's probably not on the cover of *Forbes* or *GQ*, but he wants to know he's "your man."

However, your responsibility requires a lot more than coughing up a few compliments. God also calls you to respect your husband. As a matter of fact, He specifically commands that in Ephesians 5:33. That means you respect him enough to follow his leadership. He doesn't have to be timid. He doesn't have to walk on eggshells, and he doesn't have to fear future consequences each time he makes a decision. He's able to lead knowing he has your respect. That doesn't mean you're a bystander who's looking from the outside in. Godly men always include their wives in their decisions. Godly men respect their wives enough to acknowledge their God-given gifts of wisdom and understanding. That means you can respect him without fear of being disrespected. Strengthen your husband, help him excel. You know how to nudge him to the front of the line. Empower him! Let him know you're trusting in his arms to catch you when you fall. Communicate that you believe in him.

I love it when Denise asks me to hold her hand when she's afraid of slipping or falling down. It means she believes I'm strong enough to keep her from falling. She believes in my ability to take care of her. Our culture usually highlights the men who are incredibly handsome, physically fit, or extremely wealthy, and because of our culture a lot of men struggle with feelings of inadequacy. Good men who love their wives often believe that their wives deserve something better. Wife, it's up to you to assure your husband that in your eyes he is the best. He needs to feel like a big deal to you. Not because of his salary or the cost of the gifts he gives, but because he loves you. For some of you that means you're going to have to stop belittling your husband in public. No man enjoys sitting around the table with friends while his wife airs all of his inadequacies. Those conversations not only tear him down, they announce to everyone hearing the conversation that his wife is vulnerable. She is dissatisfied with him. These conversations dishonor her husband and they also dishonor God. Unfortunately I've felt the awkwardness that's created when a husband or wife verbally expresses their marital dissatisfaction in a crowded room. Every word seems to be an attempt to plunge the knife of contempt in a little deeper. There is *never* an occasion when that is right or profitable. No one ever accomplishes anything good by verbally trashing his or her spouse. The Bible says, "Let no corrupt communication proceed from your mouth, but what is good for necessary edification, that it may impart grace to the hearers" (Ephesians 4:29). God calls us to have conversations that build one another up, to have conversations that are filled with undeserved kindness. You don't just say positive things about your spouse when he or she meets your demands, you speak edifying words to your spouse out of obedience to God.

That is a powerful rule that should be applied to all our communication. It should transcend our verbal communication and impact our physical communication as well. We don't just *speak* grace, but we also *act out* grace. Grace not only flows through our *words* but our *actions*. Grace not only finds its way into our *conversations,* it also finds its way into our *bedrooms.* Marital communication involves more than words. Sexual touch speaks volumes—especially to men. Whether you realize it or not you are sexually communicating with your spouse. You are either drawing them closer or you are pushing them farther away. "Because sex is the most intimate connection we can have with another it requires the integration of *all we are* into that sexual involvement—our love, our commitment, our integrity, our bodies, our very lives—for all our years."[27] Sexual desire is always communicated loudly and clearly. That's how affairs get started. A man knows when a woman is sexually available to him by the way she communicates with him. Men are usually keenly aware of sexual availability.

Husbands know when their wives are sexually receptive and when they're not. Your physical communication should signal that you are available to him. There are times when that will require grace, times when you welcome his attempts to be intimate and lovingly accept his inopportune desire for affection. By letting him express his desire for you, you communicate your love for him. Virtually all men want to be wanted, and they close the lines of communication when they're consistently rejected. Verbal communication and sexual communication are both important. It can't be all talking or else you're just friends, and it can't be all sex with no talking or else you will never be friends. The key is balance. Be a husband who focuses on the unique needs of your wife, and be a wife who focuses on the unique needs of your husband. There is nothing simple about grace-filled communication, but if your marriage is filled with grace, it will be filled with life. It can't get any more serious than this....grace needs to be operating in your marriage.

It takes effort and requires a deep commitment to live out the grace of God in your marriage. It takes time. Remember? It takes time! If you plan on achieving strong communication in your marriage, just know that it will never happen without investing time. Plan on the calendar of your life changing, and when it does, watch how much the life of your marriage changes.

Recently I found myself in an unfamiliar part of Chicago. Streets signs were everywhere and all of them led somewhere, but none of them were familiar to me. There were no familiar places to help me get my bearings or landmarks to use as a reference point. It was all completely strange and very unfamiliar. I could have been daring and just followed my instincts. My strategy could have been to trust my own feelings. I could have made the turns that felt right or even ones I *thought* were right. All of them led to a location. It would have been easy to end up somewhere, but I wasn't travelling to reach somewhere. I wanted to reach the right destination, and in order to do that I had to place my faith in another pastor's GPS. There we were, two men listening to the computer generated voice of a woman bossing us (I mean *helping* us) with turn by turn directions. His GPS navigated our journey from the airport to the hotel with perfect precision. Each time she gave us an instruction we responded, and eventually we heard her say the words, "Your destination is just ahead." As we drove into the parking lot of our hotel that night we both realized it was because the GPS had given us clear instructions.

So far I've given you directions but I haven't shown you a destination. I want to narrow the scope and talk out what it means to "give to your spouse inconveniently" because that is at the heart of marital effort. Unfortunately, we're living in a culture that is obsessed with convenience. Restaurants, grocery chains, and leading retailers continue to open up more outlets in an attempt to offer their customers more convenience. Technology is also being driven by people's demand for convenience. Computers have been replaced by cell phones with apps for everything. The news, weather, social networking, and even your bank account can all be conveniently accessed via your cell phone.

Sadly, this trend has created a culture of self-focused people who carry their craving for convenience into their marriages. I believe this horrible problem is one of the primary reasons America leads the world in divorce. Irreconcilable differences are commonly claimed by two people who have no issue other than they're not getting what they need from each other. I suggest radically rebelling against this trend in our culture by creating an environment of inconvenient giving in your marriage. Learn to love like Jesus! He loved without limits—He loved inconveniently.

The voices around you represent a culture of people obsessed with themselves. They are people who believe another relationship, another purchase, or reclaiming their youth by being wild and single again is going to make them happy. Their actions make me want to look them in the faces and repeat my youngest daughter's favorite word: "Really?" The only way to be truly satisfied is to give yourself to something greater than *you*. Inconvenient giving isn't convenient, but consider what you have if your spouse is just convenient. Imagine looking into the eyes of your husband or your wife and saying, "I only love you enough to do what is convenient." That would be terrible! And it's not that we aren't capable of loving inconveniently, because we are *very* capable. Loving parents embrace that as their responsibility, athletes who excel view inconvenience as necessary, small business owners view inconvenience as a way of life. So why do husbands and wives fail to go beyond convenient love? Successful marriages require extreme giving and that is inconvenient.

Regardless of how much you love your husband or wife there are times when the best of marriages aren't easy because marriage requires giving. Marriage requires that you give of yourself. It requires that you give emotionally, physically, sexually, and spiritually. Marriage draws water from all of your wells and that's why it often leaves you feeling drained. For just a moment think about these questions and then answer honestly.

- How often does your marriage inconvenience you?
- How often do you pour yourself into your spouse?
- Excluding household, parental, and work responsibilities how often do you allow yourself to be exhausted by your spouse?

- How often does the person you're married to receive the best you have to give?

Honest answers to these questions should help you evaluate your marriage and determine whether you *are* or *aren't* giving real effort. In order to get from where you are now to where you need to be you have to be willing to follow directions. Roads that lead to somewhere are all around you, but the road to a successful marriage is marked by inconvenient love.

Take a few moments to measure the level of effort you're currently dedicating to your marriage.

A Serious Reminder

"So then each of us shall give an account of himself to God" (Romans 7:12). Stop reading, stop talking, sit quietly for just a moment and imagine standing before God. Even the thought of that moment humbles me. Imagine God's eyes focusing on you as He begins to read the story of your life. He knows every detail, every intricacy. There's no running away or hiding. There's no reward for good intentions and no opportunity to reverse what's already been done. What you meant instead of what you said will be revealed. What you hid that you should have confessed will be made known. The curtains will be opened and the real you will take center stage. Every motive behind every deed will be exposed in the light of God. No excuses, no escaping. No bargaining, no convincing. We will all have to give an account to the all-knowing, all-powerful God. Our belief in the inevitability of that day should mold every aspect of our lives—including our marriages. One day all of us will stand before God and give an account for how we treated our spouses.

Husbands, you will answer to God for how well you led your homes spiritually. You will answer for your selfishness. You will answer for your attitudes, your complaining, and your manipulating. You will answer for how well you modeled the love of Christ and for whether or not your wife's relationship with *you* helped her relationship with *Him*. You will answer to God for how you treated your wife spiritually, physically, emotionally, financially, and sexually. All of that will be accounted for and everything you have not repented of will be brought to light.

Wives, you will also stand before God and give an account as well. You will answer for your words. You will answer for how you used your power as a woman. Were you demanding and manipulating or were you helpful and humble? You will answer for how supportive you were, how submissive you were. You will give an account for how well you completed your husband. Did you add to him or rebel against God's design for you and take away from him? Did you equip your husband to be the spiritual man God created him to be? Imagine the day you give an account for how you treated your husband spiritually, physically, emotionally, financially, and sexually.

For just a moment imagine answering these questions with the eyes of the all-seeing God focused only on you. Just thinking about that moment should bring all of us to tears. It should cause us to examine ourselves and be dissatisfied. It should cause us to embrace the reality that life is serious because it ends with judgment. The Bible teaches that we all have an appointment with death and after that we will be judged (Hebrews 9:27). Nothing could be more serious. True love is serious because it leads you to love your spouse in a way that pleases God, knowing that you will answer to Him. I not only love Denise for *Denise*, but I love her for *God*. He is watching, He is listening, and He is keeping the record. I should take this truth to heart. You should take this truth to heart. Love is extremely serious!

Now as a couple, stop and think about how you would feel if today were the day you had to stand before God. How many regrets would you have that you can easily identify? How serious have you been about loving your spouse? What are some of the attitudes you need to confess? What are some of the actions you need to make right before that day arrives? I strongly suggest that you take some time to talk out what you see in your heart. Talk about the areas that are most convicting. Talk about the issues that God has made you aware of and then, as a couple, *repent*. Start living opposite of who you've been, opposite of the bad behaviors that have been tolerated by both of you. Repent of the things that have torn you apart and start living toward the marriage you know God wants you to have.

If you're reading this book that means it's not too late! Stop living for the moment and start living for good-bye. Have the sobering thought that one day one of you will stand by a graveside *first*. Psalm 23 will be read, "Amazing Grace" will be sung, and you will be forced to say good-bye. That day is coming! The last thing you want is to live with regrets. The last thing you want is to lay flowers on the grave of your husband or wife and wish you had given them those flowers while he or she was alive. I've heard so many people say, "If I had only …", but they said those words too late.

The good news is that doesn't have to be you. That doesn't have to be your marriage, and that doesn't have to be your story. You still have an opportunity to write the end of your story. You can start working on what you want the last chapter to say. You *can* have a great marriage, you *can* live beyond your regrets, and you *can* start living in light of your day of accountability. You can have the marriage that other people desire to have. You can be the couple that demonstrates a Christ-like marriage in a world where people rarely see Christ. The time to discover true love is now.

Bibliography

Anderson, Neil T., and Charles Mylander. *The Christ Centered Marriage.* Ventura, CA: Regal, 1996.

Bender, Doug, and Dave Sterrett. *I Am Second.* Nashville, TN: Thomas Nelson, 2012.

Chapman, Gary. *The Four Seasons of Marriage.* Carol Stream, IL: Tyndale House Publishers, Inc., 2005.

Clarke, David. *Kiss Me Like You Mean It.* Grand Rapids, MI: Revell, 2009.

Driscoll, Mark, and Grace Driscoll. *Real Marriage the Truth About Sex, Friendship & Life Together.* Nashville, TN: Thomas Nelson, 2012.

Evans, Jimmy, and Karen Evans. *Marriage on the Rock.* Ventura, CA: Regal, 1994.

—. *Marriage on the Rock.* Ventura, CA: Regal, 2007.

Family Life. *The Art of Marriage.* Little Rock, AR: Family Life Publishing, 2011.

Field, Tiffany. "The Importance of Touch." *Touch Research Institutes from Johnson and Johnson Pediatric Institute.* 2004. http://www.baby.com/jjpi/infant-massage/The-Importance-of-Touch.pdf (accessed June 25, 2012).

George, Jim. *A Husband After God's Own Heart.* Eugene, OR: Harvest House Publishers, 2004.

Gill, John. "Exposition of the New Testament." *BibleStudyTools.com.* 1746-1748. http://www.biblestudytools.com/commentaries/gills-exposition-of-the-bible/1-timothy-2-14.html (accessed August 22, 2012).

Harley, Willard F. Jr. *Love Busters.* Grand Rapids, MI: Revell, 2008.

Jones, Lolo, interview by Bryant Gumbel. *HBO's Real Sports, Episode 182* (May 21, 2012).

Kendrick, Stephen, and Alex Kendrick. *The Love Dare.* Nashville, TN: B&H Publishing Group, 2008.

Leman, Kevin. *Sheet Music: Uncovering the Secrets of Sexual Intimacy in Marriage.* Carol Stream, IL: Tyndale House Publishers, Inc., 2003.

—. *Turn Up the Heat.* Grand Rapids, MI: Revel, 2009.

Lucado, Max. *In the Grip of Grace.* Dallas, TX: Word Publishing, 1996.

MacDonald, James. *LORD, Change My Attitude (Before It's Too Late).* Chicago, IL: Moody Press, 2001.

McIlhaney, Joe S., and Freda McKissic Bush. *Hooked.* Chicago, Il: Northfield Publishing, 2008.

McKitrick, Melanie (Miller), and Xiaonan Kou. "Charitable Giving and the Millennial Generation." *Giving USA Spotlight.* 2010. http://download.2164.net/PDF-newsletters/Giving%20USA%202010%20spotlight.pdf (accessed July 9, 2012).

Piper, John. *This Momentary Marriage (A Parable of Permanence).* Wheaton, IL: Crossway Books, 2009.

Rainey, Dennis, and Barbara Rainey. *Rekindling the Romance.* Nashville, TN: Nelson Books, 2004.

—. *Staying Close (Stopping the Drift Toward Isolation in Marriage).* Nashville, TN: Thomas Nelson, 2003.

Rosberg, Gary, and Barbara Rosberg. *The 5 Sex of Men & Women.* Carol Stream, IL: Tyndale House Publishers, Inc., 2006.

Smalley, Gary. *For Better or For Best.* Grand Rapids, MI: Zondervan Publishing House, 1988.

—. *I Promise.* Franklin, TN: Integrity Publishers, 2006.

—. *If Only He Knew.* Grand Rapids, MI: Zondervan, 1988.

Chapter Notes

Chapter 1

[1] (McKitrick and Kou 2010)

[2] (Smalley, I Promise 2006) page 205

[3] (Gill 1746-1748) These are notes from his commentary on 1Timothy 2:14.

[4] (Harley 2008) page 61. I respect the majority of this work but I strongly believe that love requires sacrifice instead of marital negotiation.

[5] (Anderson and Mylander 1996) page 77

Chapter 2

[6] (Kendrick and Kendrick 2008) page 71

[7] (Evans and Evans, Marriage on the Rock 2007) page 169

[8] (Smalley, If Only He Knew 1988) Page 124

Chapter 3

[9] (Clarke 2009) page 134

[10] (Family Life 2011) page 134

[11] (Piper 2009) page 46

[12] (Smalley, For Better or For Best 1988) page 15

[13] (Field 2004)

[14] (Driscoll and Driscoll 2012) page 38

Chapter 4

[15] (MacDonald 2001) page 71

[16] (Rainey and Rainey, Rekindling the Romance 2004) Page 37

[17] (Lucado 1996) page 151

[18] (Bender and Sterrett 2012) page 98

[19] (Driscoll and Driscoll 2012) page 93

[20] (George 2004)page 68

[21] Ibid.

[22] (Jones 2012)

[23] (Leman, Sheet Music: Uncovering the Secrets of Sexual Intimacy in Marriage 2003) page 9

[24] Ibid., page 96-97

[24] (Rainey and Rainey, Staying Close (Stopping the Drift Toward Isolation in Marriage) 2003) page 6

[25] (Family Life 2011) page 27. This is an adaptation from John Gottman's book, *Why Marriages Succeed or Fail: and How You Can Make Yours Last*. New York, New York. Simon and Schuster, 1995.

[26] (McIlhaney and Bush 2008) page 104

TIME FOR TWO

This section of the book is designed to help you have a few moments of intimate, meaningful communication. There are no wrong answers and neither of you are allowed to be offended. Take as much time as you need, and pray that through these moments together God will greatly bless your marriage.

In your own words define love.

Husband:

Wife:

List five ways you are currently serving the needs of your spouse.

Husband:

Wife:

Point out three specific ways your marriage glorifies God (makes God look great).

Husband & Wife:

Discuss the areas of selfishness in your marriage. Once you've identified those areas talk about some intentional steps to resolve those issues.

Husband & Wife:

Read Ephesians 5: 15–33 and talk about how you can revolutionize your marriage by practicing these verses.

Identify the things that cause insecurity in your marriage relationship.

Effort communicates worth and value. What immediate changes in your effort can you make to show your spouse his or her worth and value to you?

How healthy is your relationship with God and how does that impact your marriage? Also, take some time to discuss ways to affair-proof your marriage.

How sexually satisfied are you in your marriage? Frequency, passion, adventure, and desires are great discussion topics.

What is one thing you've never done sexually but you would love to?

What could you do outside of the bedroom to improve things inside of the bedroom?

Read 1 Corinthians 7: 1– 5 and discuss areas of sexual strength and weakness in your marriage.

When do you feel most loved and most secure in your marriage?

How would you complete this sentence? "I need more help with _____."

What are you doing as a couple to improve your walk with God?

Describe to your spouse the greatest lesson marriage has taught you.

Read the gospel of Luke together and identify the characteristics of Christ that you should model in your marriage.

Husbands, ask your wife: What can I do to lead you spiritually, make you feel more loved and honored?

Wives, ask your husband: What can I do to show you more love and admiration? What do you need from me?

What do you want your marriage to look like when you're old?

What area of your marriage needs to be made right before you give your account to God?

CPSIA information can be obtained at www.ICGtesting.com
Printed in the USA
BVOW012052151112

305718BV00001B/3/P

9 781462 722877